Americans All—
A Nation of Immigrants

By MURIEL STANEK
Elementary School Principal
Chicago, Illinois

CLINTON HARTMANN
Social Studies Consultant
El Paso, Texas

Consultants:

Robert Rodriguez, Director of Community Relations
El Monte Elementary School District

Israel Novoa, Executive Director
Spanish Civic Committee

BENEFIC PRESS WESTCHESTER, ILLINOIS

Contents

Library of Congress
Number 72-79637

Copyright 1972 by Benefic Press
All Rights Reserved
Printed in the United States of America

Immigrants sight the Statue of Liberty, the symbol of freedom, after a long and difficult journey.

American Immigration Begins

America has been molded by millions of immigrants. These are the people who came to live in America from other countries. The hard work of the immigrants changed a wilderness into a powerful nation. Only in America have so many different people come to live and work together. A new American culture has grown out of the mixture of many old cultures, brought by millions of immigrants. A culture is the customs, traditions, and habits of the people. Americans are proud of their old world background. But most of all, they are proud to be Americans. They are Americans first, then German, Spanish, Irish, Italian, Mexican, Polish, or Negro.

Immigration in America

Immigrants have settled in many places in the world. But nowhere, except in America, has such a large number of people from many, many different backgrounds come to live and work together. Since 1607 more than 43 million people have come to America. There are 200 million people in the United States. All of them are immigrants or descendants of immigrants.

Who were the earliest people in America?

When the early European explorers came to America, they found men living here. Anthropologists, those scientists who study the beginnings of man, believe these people came from Asia. They had come long before the explorers found the new continent, which is a great area of land. These people from Asia probably traveled in boats and came to America through Alaska and the Aleutian Islands. They probably used many of these tiny islands as stopping places in their long journey. Some of these islands have since disappeared into the ocean. Some Asians may have come by sled over the ice during the winter. Most scientists say that the people moved southward through North America and South America. All of the groups of people that remained came to be called the American Indians.

This map shows the journey of the Asians who came to America through the Aleutian Islands.

European explorers came to North America long after the Indians. New trade routes were being sought all over the world by explorers from Spain, Portugal, Italy, France, and England. They hoped to find new land and riches. They sailed for Asia, Africa, and Australia. It is little wonder that some explorers finally came upon the North American continent.

Who were the Vikings?

The Vikings from northern Europe are believed to be the first to have explored and settled in North America. Sailing across the Atlantic Ocean, they arrived in Iceland and Greenland, islands in the Atlantic Ocean. This happened at least five hundred years before Christopher Columbus came to North America. It is said that Leif Ericson, one of the Viking leaders, sailed down along the coast as far as Newfoundland. He called the country Vinland.

There are several possible reasons why the Viking settlements did not survive. Stories tell of fierce battles between the natives and the Vikings. These stories of historic heroes of the Vikings are called sagas. These stories tell about the gods and heroes of the Vikings. Facts show that there was a big change of climate in Greenland after 1200 B.C. The very cold climate might have driven the Vikings out. Problems at home in Norway also might have caused them to leave their settlements in the new world and return to their mother country. Whatever the reason, the Viking colonies disappeared and were forgotten.

Leif Ericson and the Vikings were the earliest explorers in North America. The colonies they established, however, soon disappeared.

Both Leif Ericson and Christopher Columbus brought men of many different nationalities on their voyages to the New World.

It was not until after Christopher Columbus' famous voyage of 1492 that many explorers and settlers left for the new land. North America was never to be forgotten again.

From the beginning, America was to become the land with a great mixture of population. Columbus, an Italian, had people from many backgrounds on board his ship. Spaniards, English, Irish, Portuguese, Jews, and a Negro are said to have sailed as part of the crew on that famous voyage. Thus, the model for America's future population was begun nearly five hundred years ago.

The first English settlement was on the James River in Virginia.

What effect did the explorers have on America?

The earliest explorers came to America by chance. Later adventurers planned their trips and got <u>charters</u>, written permission to settle the land. The Spaniards were the most active early explorers in America. They explored the southwest part of the country all the way to California. They also settled in Florida. There, in 1565, they founded St. Augustine, our oldest city. The influence of the early Spaniards is still seen in the architecture, old missions, names of families, and words that are used, such as rodeo and pueblo.

The English <u>migration</u>, or movement to another land, was later than the Spanish. Humphrey Gilbert led the first English voyage. He arrived at Newfoundland in 1583. Some of the English hoped to find gold. But the land did not give them the treasures they expected. Instead, they found the rich soil and forests of the northeast part of what is now the United States. They found land that gave them only a hope of wealth. This land needed hard work. Instead of taking gold back to England, they returned to the new land with more people. After many failures, an English colony was finally settled in Virginia in 1607. Virginia Dare was the first child of European parents to be born in America.

10

Besides having a powerful navy, England had strong colonies in America. They became the largest and strongest group in the new land. In 1588, England's ships defeated the Spanish Armada in a naval battle in the English Channel. Spain's place in the new land was weakened.

The French started colonies around the time the English settled their first permanent colony in Virginia. Most French colonies were along the Great Lakes. However, many of the French wanted the the fur trade more than permanent settlements. They moved along the Great Lakes and controlled much of the land nearby. By working with the Indians, they hoped they could get rich with their fur trading. It was difficult to control such a large area of land. A disagreement between the English and French led to war. The French were defeated in the colonies. Thus, the English colonists who wanted a permanent settlement won the war.

By 1754 the population of the colonies had reached more than one and a half million people. About one-fourth of the people were Negroes. In the New England Colonies, most of the people were English. In the Middle Colonies, the people were mostly Dutch, German, Irish, Swedish, French, Negro, and Scotch-Irish. The Scotch-Irish were people from Scotland who had lived in northern Ireland. In the Southern Colonies, there were English along the coast and Scotch-Irish and German in the western part of these colonies. A large number of Negroes were in the South as slaves. Soon other groups would arrive to help build America.

Father Junipero Serra established the first mission at San Diego, California, in 1769.

What part did the Negro play in the settling of America?

The first Negro arrived in America in 1619. In the following years, thousands of Negro slaves were brought from Africa and the West Indies. During the 1700's probably 200,000 Negro slaves were brought to America. Most of them were sent to the Southern Colonies. The Negroes were not immigrants in the same way as Europeans. They were settlers, too, but they did not choose to come to America. Negroes were captured in Africa and sold as slaves. They did not have the same hopes for the future as the other settlers. Many Negroes cleared the land and worked in the fields. They helped make the American way of life.

How did the new nation grow?

The colonies soon had many people with different languages and customs. At one time it seemed that the new land would have three languages—Spanish, French, and English. The English colonies were the strongest. Most of the other colonies soon followed the English customs. The language, the law, and the government were from the English tradition, or custom. While most customs were English, each group of people added their own customs to the new land in which they lived.

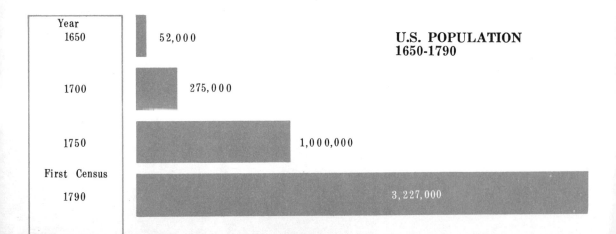

U.S. POPULATION
1650-1790

Year	
1650	52,000
1700	275,000
1750	1,000,000
First Census 1790	3,227,000

The graph shows the percentages of the different nationalities in America in 1790.

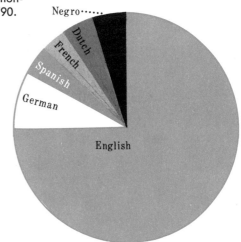

The colonial population was over 50,000 in 1650. By 1700 it was 250,000. The first <u>census</u>, taken in 1790, was three million. The census is the official counting of the people in a country. At that time 75 percent of the people were English. The Germans were 8 percent of the population. Smaller groups of people were the Dutch, French, Spanish, and Swedish. There were an additional 750,000 Negroes living mostly in the South.

Why did the Europeans come to America?

After the American Revolution in 1783, few people came to the United States. Those who came now were mostly from England and Ireland. With fewer new settlers, there was time for the young nation to develop an American <u>nationality</u>. Nationality is a feeling of belonging to a nation. The people of the new United States did not belong to any other country. Instead, they had their own country. The American Revolution had made them free. Now, they were here to stay. A spirit of pride in America grew as the ties with England were finally broken. The feeling of being an American became stronger.

A great number of immigrants began to come to the United States in 1815. It started one of the largest migrations of people ever known in history. From then to World War I, thirty million people came to make their homes in the United States. Most of them came from European countries.

There were many reasons why people left their homes to come to the new land. In Europe, great changes were taking place. The Industrial Revolution brought new ways of working and living. Many kinds of machines were invented. These machines were built to produce things for people. Before this time, clothing and other things for everyday living were made by hand. Now they could be made in shorter time and at less cost. Machines could do the work of hundreds of people. Thousands of trained workmen lost their jobs. Many people left their old country and came to find work in the United States of America.

There were many other reasons why people left Europe. Some came to the United States to find freedom from religious and political wars. Others came because of the Great Famine in the 1840's. Potatoes were the main food for many poor people of Europe. The Potato Blight, a disease that killed the potato plants, caused a shortage of food. Many of the people of Europe were starving. Their only hope was to come to America.

What hardships did the people have on their way to America?

Making the long trip to America was not easy. Almost everything they owned had to be left behind. Friends were left behind. It usually took two or three months to cross the Atlantic Ocean in a sailing ship. The immigrants needed great courage to make the long, hard trip.

Immigrants came to the United States to seek new and better jobs. The factories of the Industrial Revolution needed workers.

The most common way of travel for immigrants was in steerage. They could not afford anything better.

Many of the immigrants left small villages and farms in Europe. It was sad for them to say good-bye to their relatives and friends. Most of them would never see their "old country" again. They wanted to come to the new land. But it was hard to leave the things they knew and loved.

The trip was too hard for the old people and those who were not strong. They had to stay behind. People had to save money for the trip. Men would work many years to save enough money to buy a ticket. Sometimes the father would go to America without his family. Then he would work hard in America and send for them when he had saved enough money to pay for their trip. Some American companies would pay their way if the people would work for them for a certain amount of time.

The families who started the long trip had many other problems. Sometimes the ship was late in sailing. People often waited days on the docks. If they had enough money, they could stay in a boarding house. But most people could not afford this extra expense. Once they were aboard the ship, there were more hardships. Immigrants usually traveled in the steerage, a place below deck. It was cheaper traveling there than on the upper level. Usually, there were four hundred to a thousand people on the ship. It was crowded. The light from the lanterns was poor. There was little or no heat. Often there was little food or water.

How did the immigrants travel?

The immigrants carried everything in boxes and bags. Some people had small trunks. Each carried a few important things from their old home. Some had tablecloths, some had one or two pieces of glassware, some even had home-made pillows. The women wore shawls to cover their heads and shoulders. Babies were wrapped in patchwork quilts.

The immigrants carried food to last for part of the voyage. They had sausage, cheese and bread. Extra food cost too much money. The poor food, lack of fresh air, and the rough voyage made many people sick.

This way of traveling was very poor. In 1848, a law was passed making ships carry enough food and stoves for the people. By 1860 steamships were used. Now the voyage took only two weeks. America was becoming the land of hope and dreams for thousands of new-comers. The first person to see land would call out "America, America!" Everyone would hurry to see the new land. They would stand on tiptoes to see above the others. Each one was excited to get his first look at America. The first thing most of the people saw was the Statue of Liberty. Soon they would sail into New York harbor. Some cried. Some smiled. Some gave prayers of thanks. It was a time of great happiness as each person stepped onto American soil. Often friends or relatives met them in New York.

This Italian family came to America with only the belongings they could carry.

WHAT DO YOU THINK?

1. Why did the explorers come to the new land? What did they find when they arrived?
2. Why did the European immigrants come to America? Was it the best thing for them to do? Why?
3. What would be the hardest thing about the trip?
4. What would be the best thing?
5. Why is the English language used by Americans instead of Spanish, French, or German?

6. Why would the Statue of Liberty have special meaning for most immigrants?
7. Why are American tourists interested in seeing the Statue of Liberty in New York?
8. Many blacks were brought to America as slaves. Did they have the same hopes as other immigrants for the future? Why?
9. Why would it take courage for a family to leave Europe and come to America?
10. How are traveling conditions for today's immigrant families different from those of the 1880's?

11. How did the Indians get to North America?
12. Do you think the early settlers and colonists changed American culture more than did the early explorers? Why?
13. What was the Industrial Revolution? Why did it affect immigration to America?

This drawing depicts a scene in 1850 at Castle Garden.

Immigrants in the New Nation

What problems did they meet?

When the ships arrived in the New York harbor, immigrants had to start a new life. Some had relatives to greet them and take them home. These were fortunate people because they had some place to go. They had someone to help them until they could find work and a place to live. Some had to learn the language. Others were all alone in the new land. Thousands of immigrants stayed for a short time at Castle Garden. This was a large center in New York that tried to help immigrants find jobs and places to live. The first place on American soil for many millions of immigrants was Ellis Island. This island in New York harbor was the place where the immigrants first entered. Here they had to check in with the American government. Ellis Island was established as an immigrant center in 1892. The American government stopped using the island in 1954. It is thought that about 20 million immigrants entered through Ellis Island.

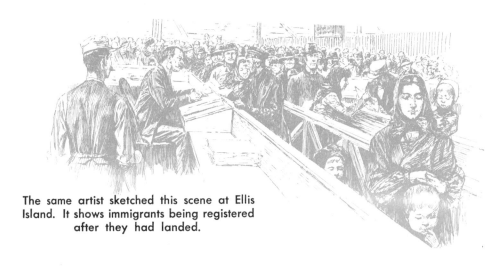

The same artist sketched this scene at Ellis Island. It shows immigrants being registered after they had landed.

Why did neighborhoods of immigrants grow in the cities?

The immigrants traveled to all parts of the country. Some had made arrangements before they left the old country to work on railroads, in the mines, or in a factory. Others planned to work on farms.

Immigrants usually settled near their friends or relatives. Here they could speak their own language and follow their old world customs. Towns and cities had neighborhoods with large immigrant groups. The Germans usually lived in one part of the city. The Irish lived in another part. The Swedes, Italians and Polish lived in other parts of the city.

Local food stores kept foods that immigrants used in their old country. Special sausage, cheese, oils, pastries, and spices were sold. Many cities had newspapers in foreign languages. Special holidays and religious feasts were celebrated by each group.

What were the daily lives of the immigrants like?

The immigrants had a hard life, but they had fun, too. Friends and relatives played cards or visited over a cup of coffee or tea. Someone always had a violin or an accordion. They played gay tunes from the old country. The <u>polka</u> and the <u>mazurka</u> were always favorite dances of the Slavic peoples.

19

After an immigrant family had arrived and settled in America, the father often entertained his children with stories about the old country.

Families had their happy hours in the evening. Mothers usually knitted and mended clothes. Often the family worked together on things for the house. Sometimes they sat around the kitchen table and made patchwork quilts. A kerosene lamp was their only light. A coal burning stove was their only heat. Sometimes they picked goose feathers from the geese they had raised in the back yard. These made soft, warm pillows and down covers for cold nights.

In many families when the children came home from school with their books, the children would teach English to their parents.

If the father worked in the stockyards or on construction jobs, the children cleaned the mud from his heavy boots.

Restful and quiet times were typical of the evening activities. Sometimes the father smoked his foot-long pipe. Children liked to fill his pipe with tobacco. They watched him blow rings of smoke as he told stories and folktales from the old country. Sometimes the stories went on and on. The children became sleepy. They could not stay awake. Their parents would tuck them into bed with the home-made feather pillows and down covers.

Immigrants selected many different kinds of work. Some worked in factories, some in the arts, and some in farming.

How did the immigrants earn their living?

Many immigrants found places to work in the growing city factories. New York, Chicago, and Boston had large immigrant populations. Some newcomers brought their work skills to the new land. There were carpenters, locksmiths, tailors, cooks, barbers and many others with trades that were useful. Other immigrants were unskilled workers who did laboring jobs on railroads, in mines, and in the stockyards.

The immigrants who came between the 1850's and 1930's were less skilled. Many were poor peasants, farm laborers, or owners of small farms from southern Europe. Most of these immigrants were not frontiersmen or pioneer farmers. They could not use a gun or rifle needed in the western land. Instead, they took over farms from those who were moving farther west.

Many immigrant farmers were very poor. They had spent all the money they had for the trip to this country. Some bought a few acres of land with their savings. Others used their right to home-stead, which meant the land was given to those who settled it. Many of the farms in the western United States were started by immigrants who homesteaded the land.

Jane Addams began language classes for immigrants at Hull House. Classes were held at Hull House until they were taken over by the Chicago Board of Education.

Many people found homes in very crowded, poor sections of the cities. Settlement houses were started in cities where large numbers of immigrants lived. Jane Addams began Hull House in Chicago. Lillian Wald's House on Henry Street was started in New York City. Both of these settlement houses became famous throughout the world. Immigrants, young and old, were helped by the workers in these neighborhood settlement houses. They learned about their new country and made friends with their new neighbors. The settlement houses offered a place for recreation. Thousands of immigrants were taught English as they studied for their citizenship examinations. It was always a proud day when the new citizens would give the Pledge of Allegiance to the American flag.

What were the great movements of immigration?

The English were the largest group in America from 1600 to 1800. After that people from other parts of the world came. Many hoped for better jobs. Most of all they wanted the freedom that America offered.

People came to America in four great movements. From 1815 to 1860, most of the immigrants were from western Europe. The immigrants were from England, Scotland, Wales, Ireland, and south-western Germany. About seven and a half million came at that time. A small number of Chinese came, too. During the Civil War immigration stopped.

The second great wave of immigration began at the close of the Civil War in 1865. This movement lasted until 1890. Some western Europeans still came, but now northern Europeans came, too. These new-comers were from Norway, Sweden, Denmark, and Finland. About eight million people made the journey to America during that time.

The largest movement of immigrants came between 1890 and 1924. More than twenty million people arrived in America. People still came from western and northern Europe. Now, many came from eastern and southern Europe, too. Czechs, Slovaks, Hungarians, Serbs, Poles, Russians, and Ukranians came in large numbers.

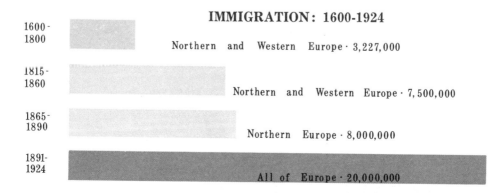

IMMIGRATION: 1600-1924

1600-1800	Northern and Western Europe · 3,227,000
1815-1860	Northern and Western Europe · 7,500,000
1865-1890	Northern Europe · 8,000,000
1891-1924	All of Europe · 20,000,000

Nearly two million Jews from eastern Europe and four million peasants from Italy came to America, too. Other countries from which immigrants came were Rumania, Greece, Turkey, Albania, and Syria. By 1900 the movement had become world-wide. Japanese, Filipinos, East Indians, and Mexicans also came to start new homes in the United States. People from all over the world looked toward America for a happier and better life. They came from almost every country in the world.

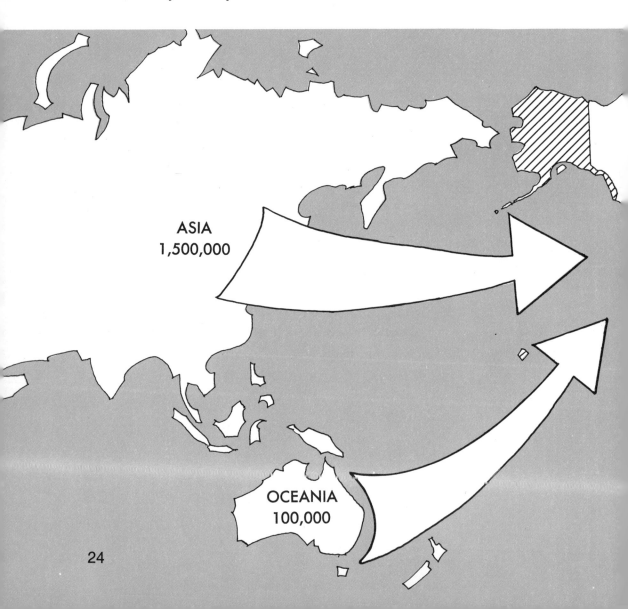

ASIA
1,500,000

OCEANIA
100,000

The last great movement of immigrants came between 1945 and 1960. This movement was different from the other movements. World War II had ended. During the war many people went to other countries for safety. These people are called <u>refugees</u>. At the end of the war many refugees came to America. Then, too, during the war many soldiers married European girls. When they returned, they brought their new wives home to the United States.

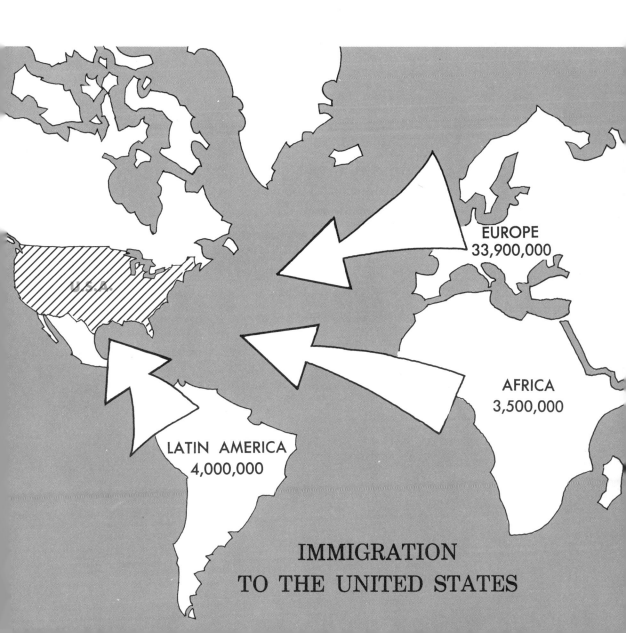

EUROPE
33,900,000

AFRICA
3,500,000

U.S.A

LATIN AMERICA
4,000,000

IMMIGRATION
TO THE UNITED STATES

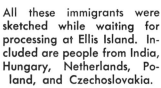

All these immigrants were sketched while waiting for processing at Ellis Island. Included are people from India, Hungary, Netherlands, Poland, and Czechoslovakia.

Most immigrants became citizens of the United States. Yet, some of their "old country" customs are still followed by their children and grandchildren. The mixture of old world and new world culture gives America a special feeling. Americans are different in color, religion, background, and customs. These differences have caused many problems for the people in the United States. People of different races do not always like one another. People of different religions do not always like one another. And people of different nationalities do not always like one another. A large problem in the United States today is how to get people of different races to learn to live together peacefully.

Why were immigration laws passed?

Not all of the Americans liked the immigrants. As early as 1830, people called nativists tried to stop others from coming to the United States. They wanted only native Americans to live here.

Angry feelings toward the Irish Catholics and other "foreign intruders" were felt in the early 1850's. One of these groups was called the "Know-Nothings." They got their name because they kept their activities secret and would not answer any questions. In 1856 they were very powerful and supported Millard Fillmore for President of the United States. He lost the election, but he received twenty-five percent of the votes. The "Know-Nothings" soon disappeared. Their ideas, however, have continued to the present day.

Who did the first immigration laws affect?

During the next twenty years there were other groups who believed there were too many immigrants. Finally, the first immigration law was passed in 1882. This law would not let mentally ill people or those who had been in prison come to the United States. This law also would not let Chinese come for ten years.

IMMIGRATION LAWS IN THE UNITED STATES

1862 — NO Chinese, prostitutes, convicts

1882 — NO insane, epileptics, polygamists

1891 — NO beggars, paupers, anarchists

1917 — NO Hindus, illiterates, alcoholics

1921 — Temporary quota law

1924 — Permanent quota law (NO Asians)

1929 — NO stowaways, vagrants, public charges

1940 — All immigrants must be fingerprinted

1950 — NO Communists or subversives

1952 — Small number of Asians allowed under quota law

1965 — Quota system ended

This shows part of a Chinese language newspaper that is published every day in the United States.

選舉費餘款補回獻款人

一百五十萬元云。

芝城不分派別，擁護達里競選連任第四屆市長委員會，於本年四月四日，選舉市長前，曾向各方籌募擁護達里競選費，計共贊助選舉費人四百九十三名，得款七萬三千元，但選舉完成後，僅費款六萬四千二百九十二元，尚餘八千七百六十七元，故現將餘款按名每人補回百分之十二云

About two thousand Chinese had come to America between 1850 and 1882. Labor was needed in gold mining camps and in building the railroads across the country. The Chinese worked hard for very little money. They were welcome to work as laborers and cooks. However, when the work was finished, there were few jobs. Americans were afraid the Chinese would take their work. Often the only work allowed the Chinese was cooking and washing. They were suspicious, too, of the Chinese because their ways were different from the European customs. The neighborhood in big cities where the Chinese lived was called Chinatown. Here they kept the mysterious old Chinese customs. Angry feelings toward the Chinese grew. The Chinese Exclusion Act of 1882 stopped the Chinese from coming to the United States.

Who was affected by later immigration laws?

Dislike for the new immigrants was growing. Another law was passed in 1891 which required immigrants to pass a medical test. Still another law in 1903 kept out those who would not make good citizens. By 1917 new immigrants had to read and write.

Americans did not like large numbers of southern and eastern Europeans coming to the United States. In 1890, about 80 percent of the immigrants were from northern and western Europe. Thirty years later only 23 percent were from northern and western Europe. The other 77 percent were from southern and eastern Europe. Americans worried about these many new immigrants. Most of them were poor peasants with little education. Americans looked down on their customs and religions and thought they would not help our country. They wanted to keep these immigrants out of the United States. They thought the country would be ruined if immigration were allowed to continue and people from southern and eastern Europe were allowed to come to America.

After the quota law of 1921, many southern and eastern Europeans were turned away from the United States.

A <u>quota</u> law was passed in 1921 to limit the number of immigrants to the United States. The law allowed only 357,000 people to come each year. This law favored those immigrants from northern and western Europe. Immigration for each country was limited to 3 percent of the number of that nationality living in the United States in 1910. Most Americans were from northern and western Europe. Thus, more people from northern and western Europe could continue coming to the United States. But England, Sweden, and Germany had become industrialized. There were many new jobs and plenty of food. People did not want to leave these countries now.

However, there were fewer people from southern and eastern Europe living in the United States. The quota law said that few new immigrants could come from these places. But these people were very poor and had little hope for the future. They wanted to come to America to make a better life. But few could come because of the quota law. Many wanted so badly to come to America that they would smuggle themselves into the United States.

What did the National Origin Act mean?

In 1924 another immigration law was passed. It was called the National Origin Act. Now only 150,000 people could come to the United States each year. Immigration was made even more difficult for southern and eastern Europeans.

England had the largest quota, 65,000. But less than half that number of people wanted to come to America. From Italy, only 4,000 immigrants could come under the quota. But 137,000 Italians wanted to come to America. The quota did not let many others come from countries in southern and eastern Europe. America no longer opened its doors to the poor and needy of Europe. Some people waited years for their name to be reached on the quota. Others lost all hope of coming to the United States.

The National Origin Act of 1924 made it still more difficult for eastern and southern Europeans to come to America.

What recent changes in the laws have helped the immigrant?

After World War II, there were some changes. Many people in Europe lost their homes during the war. In 1952 the law was changed. These war refugees and orphans were allowed to come to the United States, but the quota was kept.

President Kennedy wanted Congress to pass a new law that would end this quota. Congress considered it for a long time. Finally a new law was passed in 1965 which ended the quotas. President Johnson signed the bill into law in front of the Statue of Liberty. The old law was unfair. From now on the immigrants will be admitted because of their work skills. More people who want to come to the United States are now welcome. It does not matter from which country they come. Relatives of a United States citizen may come too. However, there are still some limitations so that Americans will not be put out of jobs to make room for new-comers. Once again, America has opened its doors to many who look for a new and better life. Once again, immigrants can come to the United States.

President Johnson talks about the new law that ended the quota system. He signed the law at the Statue of Liberty.

WHAT DO YOU THINK?

1. Why did people from the same country often live in the same kinds of communities in America?
2. What do you think living conditions were like in the old immigrant neighborhoods?
3. Why were the big cities good places for the immigrants to find work?

4. If you had been one of the early settlers in America, what kind of work would you have looked for? If you were interested in farming, how might you have gotten land?
5. Why is it said that all Americans come from immigrant backgrounds? Do you think this is true?
6. Why was there trouble between the new immigrants and other American workers fifty years ago?
7. Why were community centers such as Hull House important to the new immigrants?

8. What is the difference between an immigrant and a refugee?
9. What does it mean to become a naturalized citizen? How does one become a naturalized citizen?
10. What is meant by a quota? Why were quotas used?
11. Why were some quotas unfair to certain groups of people?

Immigration from Northern and Western Europe

Most of the people who first came to the United States were from northern and western Europe. Of these, the English were the largest group. Many of them settled on the east coast. Later, they moved throughout the country. It was very easy for the English to move and settle in other parts of the new land because they had no language problems. Some nationality groups stayed only in places where their own language was spoken by their neighbors.

The English influenced many things in the new land. The English had the largest influence in America. They gave America its language, the ideas for its laws, and many of its customs. They prepared America for the great movements of immigrants which were to come later. But people from other countries in northern and western Europe also influenced the growth of America.

34

Immigrants often wrote letters to their friends and relatives in the old country. They told how wonderful it was in America.

How did the people hear about America?

American ships brought grain to starving Ireland and other needy countries. Many Europeans began hearing about a promising place called "America". News from friends and relatives sometimes made the new land sound more wonderful than it really was. Some people believed that America had streets made of gold. Others thought that everyone could get rich overnight in the new land of America.

The "America Fever" spread quickly from one town to another. Sometimes a letter from a relative in America would cause a whole village to want to go to America. Letters from America were printed in the newspapers and read in churches. Families and friends would gather together for news from the United States. They hoped the letters would contain money or tickets to America.

America was growing and spreading westward. Labor was needed. American businessmen went to Europe to find workers for the ships, mines, railroads, and construction companies. They made the work sound easy. America seemed like a dream to the poor Europeans. Many people in Europe needed work. America needed labor. Thus, the immigration movement grew.

What did the Irish give to America?

Most immigrant groups were able to find jobs like those they had in Europe. Farmers worked as farmers. The shopkeepers and factory workers looked for the same kind of work they had in the old country. However, many Irish farmers were too poor to look for land to farm in America or to start a business. They stayed mainly in cities along the eastern coast where they could get work quickly as laborers.

Some Irish immigrants came to this country as <u>indentured servants</u>. This means that they agreed to work for a number of years in exchange for their passage to America. In the earlier years of our country, colonial newspapers often advertised when Irish servants were to be sold. After a few years, the debt was paid. The employer then let the servant go, giving him a small amount of money, usually less than one hundred dollars. The freed servant then looked for a job for which he would be paid.

The Irish worked as ditchdiggers and construction workers. Many Irishmen also worked on the railroads, in coal mines, and in factories, while the women worked as servants. Contractors often hired the Irish immigrants off the ships as they landed in the New York port. The new immigrants were paid less than the

These letters from America were passed around until everyone in the town or village knew the latest news from America. Usually these letters told only the good side of life in America.

Americans. Sometimes the Irish immigrants replaced other workers because it was cheaper to hire the newcomers. This often caused bad feelings between the Irish and other Americans.

The Irish workers who found jobs in mines found the working conditions very poor. Men were hurt or killed because there were few safety laws. The damp, dark mines, together with long working hours, caused many men to die at an early age.

Secret societies were formed among the laborers. They terrorized the mine bosses to force them to improve working conditions.

One of these groups was called the Molly Maguires. No one knew who the members of the Molly Maguires were except the members themselves. Fighting and fear grew. A detective worked to expose the Molly Maguires. Their power ended about 1880.

The labor movement formed during this time began to grow, and working conditions improved. The new United Mine Workers of America was recognized by the mine management and bosses. Its president was an Irishman, John Mitchell. Leaders for the mine workers worked with the mine owners on new safety rules, wages, and working conditions.

This union membership certificate shows some jobs done by miners in the 1880's.

These men used their union to strike for an eight-hour workday.

The union movement grew and affected many industries. One Irishman who became famous in the labor movement is George Meany. He began as a plumber and became the president of the American Federation of Labor.

As the Irish found steady jobs, they could live in one place. In their communities, small Catholic churches were soon built. The church was a place where all the Irish immigrants felt they really belonged. The Irish formed their own tightly-knit communities in such cities as Boston, Philadelphia, and New York.

Many young Irishmen began going into politics. New York City elected its first Irish mayor, William R. Grace, in 1880. In time, the Irish became firemen, policemen, teachers, writers, business-men, and priests. Catholic schools and universities were started by sons and grandsons of Irishmen. By 1900 a large part of big-city government was headed by Irish politicians.

Who were some outstanding Irish immigrants and descendents of immigrants?

People of Irish descent have become very well-known in many areas of American life ever since our earliest history.

Two signers of the Declaration of Independence were Matthew Thornton of New Hampshire and George Taylor of Pennsylvania. Both had come from Ireland and spent time as indentured servants. Another Irish-born signer of the

"Standing Lincoln" was made by Saint-Gaudens.

Declaration of Independence was James Smith. He became a lawyer and later a judge in Pennsylvania.

Eugene O'Neill was one of America's greatest playwrights. He won the Nobel prize for literature in 1936. He was the son of an Irish immigrant who came to America after the potato famine.

Augustus Saint-Gaudens came to America from Dublin, Ireland. He became a famous artist. In Chicago's Lincoln Park is his statue of the "Standing Lincoln." Another of his statues is of Robert Shaw, a Civil War colonel. It stands in Boston.

Victor Herbert, another Irish immigrant, was famous both as composer and conductor. He wrote more than forty operettas, or short operas with gay music. "Naughty Marietta" and "Babes in Toyland" are the best known.

John McCormack was a great Irish singer. He sang many of the famous Irish songs, such as "My Wild Irish Rose," and "When Irish Eyes Are Smiling." He often sang with the great opera companies such as the Boston, Chicago, and Metropolitan operas. John McCormack became a United States citizen in 1919.

Louis H. Sullivan was one of America's first great modern architects. His work was an example for many young architects to study. Some of the buildings designed by Louis Sullivan still stand as a reminder of the work of this great artist.

Many people of Irish descent went into politics. Al Smith was governor of New York twice and was the first Irishman to run for President of the United States. However, he was defeated in 1928 by Herbert Hoover. At that time there were strong feelings against having a Catholic President. These fears and prejudices were finally overcome in the 1960 election of President John F. Kennedy. The great-grandson of an Irish immigrant became the 35th President of the United States.

Today, many men and women of Irish descent are in important places in government, education, religion, business, law, science, sports, and the theater. There are more than 20 million Americans with Irish ancestry. Saint Patrick's Day is an important Irish-American holiday in the United States. Annual St. Patrick's Day parades in many large cities give the Irish a chance to show their great pride in their heritage. The day is enjoyed by many.

This shows a scene from Victor Herbert's "Babes in Toyland."

Although the people who came to America from Ireland learned to live in and love their new country, they kept many of their old songs and stories. One song, which told the feelings of these immigrants as they left their native land, was:

Farewell ye green hills and verdant valleys,
Where I with my sweetheart did often rove,
Where I vowed her I'd never leave her,
Whilst walking sweetly through each silent grove.
But times are changing and crops are failing,
and causing thousands to go away,
In deep emotion to cross the ocean,
To seek their fortunes in America (y).

WHAT WOULD YOU DO?

Suppose you were John Mitchell fighting for better conditions for mine workers in 1895. Many men are dying because of poor working conditions. Others die of lung disease. There is no insurance for their families.

1. What would you say to the mine owners at a meeting?
2. How could you make the mine owners understand that better working conditions would help make greater profits for them?
3. What suggestions would you make to improve conditions for miners and their families?
4. What evidence would you show the mine owners to make them understand the poorness of the working conditions?
5. What would you say at a meeting of mine workers following a mine cave-in, in which ten men were killed?

Alexander Graham Bell is shown here in the studio where he invented the telephone.

Who were outstanding Americans from England and Scotland?

Many people came to America from Scotland during colonial times. Seven signers of the Declaration of Independence came from this country that is north of England. America has had presidents, generals, scientists, and leaders in many other fields who have been proud of their Scottish heritage while helping America.

Andrew Carnegie (1837-1919) was a famous Scottish immigrant. Carnegie came to the United States at the age of thirteen. He found a job which paid $1.20 a week. When he grew older, he organized a steel-producing company. By 1900 it was the largest steel company in the country.

When Carnegie retired, he sold the Carnegie Steel Company. It has kept growing as the United States Steel Corporation. It is now the largest steel company in the world. Carnegie wanted to help his new country. During his life he gave millions of dollars for schools and libraries.

The Scotsman, Alexander Graham Bell, was an inventor who experimented with electricity. As he was trying to send telegraph messages to a helper in the next room, he spilled acid on his clothes. His voice went over the wire. The telephone was invented. The Bell Telephone Company was started the next year. Today the telephone is a very important means of communication.

Gilbert Stuart was the son of immigrants from Scotland. He was a great artist. He painted many famous people such as George Washington and John Adams.

Stephen Foster was the child of Scotch-Irish immigrants. His music was much loved. Among his songs were "My Old Kentucky Home" and "Oh Susanna."

Bowdoin College Museum of Art, Brunswick, Maine
Stuart also painted Thomas Jefferson.

The English have probably contributed more to American culture than any other group. The majority of the people of the United States have some English heritage in their backgrounds. Our laws, language, and many customs are based on those of the English. The greatest English influence on America was during the colonial days and in the early nineteenth century.

An outstanding contributor to America's government was Thomas Paine. He came to America in 1774. He wrote *Common Sense*, which is known to historians as a plea for our independence.

Great men of science and mathematics have come here from England to live. Some became teachers in universities and others did research. One of these was Dr. William Shockley who directed research for making the transistors which are so widely-used today. One American, George Eastman, bought an English photographic factory in order to get one man to come to work for him. C. E. Kenneth Mees stayed with him for more than forty years as director of the Kodak Research Laboratories.

These ladies were striking for better pay. Our modern "Women's Lib" movement would not be new to them!

Three architects who will be remembered for their work are Benjamin Latrobe, Richard Upjohn, and Calvert Vaux. Latrobe re-designed the Capitol and the White House in Washington, D.C. after damage from the War of 1812. Upjohn designed several of the churches in New York, including the beautiful Trinity Church. Vaux designed the Metropolitan Museum of Art and the Museum of Natural History, which are in New York City.

Two English women who became well-known in America were Mary Mortimer and Anna Howard Shaw. Both worked many years for equal rights for women. Mary Mortimer started the Milwaukee Female College in 1851. She also helped create the American Women's Education Association. These women were two of the many who worked for the right of women to vote.

44

Anna Shaw had the kind of life that is hard for us to imagine. She was born in England in 1847. By the age of twelve, she and her family were pioneers in northern Michigan, where her father had a farm of 360 acres. They lived in a log cabin with a dirt floor and no glass in the windows. Life was very difficult, especially with the fear of an Indian attack at any moment. Anna spent as much time reading as she could and became determined to go to college. Very few girls in those days went to college. At the age of fifteen, she became a teacher in the tiny school near her home. She was paid two dollars a week.

When the Civil War started in 1861, Anna's father and brothers joined the Union forces. This left Anna, her mother, and her sisters to run the farm. It was not until the end of the war, in 1865, that Anna could begin to save money for college.

Through hard work, Anna Shaw finally achieved her dream. She became a doctor, a Methodist minister, and a public speaker. She worked the rest of her life to improve the rights of women.

WHAT WOULD YOU DO?

In 1920 American women won the right to vote. Answer the questions as Anna might have.

1. Why do you work for women's rights rather than as a doctor?
2. If women in your native country of England can't vote, why do you think American women should be able to?
3. Women don't understand politics. How could they choose their candidates wisely?
4. What can women do to learn more about elections and government in order to vote wisely?

Faneuil Hall is still used for debates.

What did the French contribute to America?

The French Huguenots began coming to the new world in the 1660's because they wanted freedom of religion. Many were skilled workers and shopkeepers. They settled throughout the East. Paul Revere was a Huguenot. He was born in Boston, but his parents had come from France. Probably the most famous Frenchman in history was the Marquis de Lafayette. Although he kept his French citizenship, he joined the American colonists in their fight for independence from England. He died in 1834.

Shipbuilding was an important industry in young America. In 1688 Gabriel Bernon came to Boston from France to start a shipyard. He built a fleet of ships that carried products to many places.

Andre Faneuil also settled in Boston and became a successful merchant and shipowner. In later years a nephew of his, Pierre, gave that city the building now known as Faneuil Hall. It became a meeting place for protests against England. It has been called the "cradle of liberty."

Pierre Charles L'Enfant served as a Major of Engineers in the War for Independence. Later he was asked to plan the new capital city for the United States. His plan showed his confidence in America's ability to grow greater in years to come.

46

E. I. DuPont, right, founded a large chemical company. James Audubon painted the picture, far right, which helped make him America's most famous nature painter.

The chemical industry was started in this country by E. I. du Pont, who came to America in 1800. The Du Pont company grew and grew. Today it is one of the largest and most successful companies in the United States.

John Audubon (1785-1851) was also from France. Audubon was very interested in studying bird life. He traveled all over the United States studying and drawing birds in their natural surroundings. As an artist and a naturalist, this immigrant helped show people everywhere the beauty of birds in America. His work is still accepted today as being authoritative on American bird life. In 1905, long after he died, the National Audubon Society was formed. Its purpose is the protection and conservation of nature and wildlife. The children's clubs have many members.

Lily Pons was born in Cannes, France. She became an American citizen in 1940, and became famous in her new country as a leading soprano in the opera. Her singing added delight and beauty to the Metropolitan Opera Company for many years.

The French had a great influence on American life. French-Americans are found in education, science, the arts, and industry. They are especially well-known for their excellent work in clothing fashions and cooking.

For eleven years, Lilly Dache worked and planned to make a fairy-tale wish come true. That wish was to leave her native France and live in America. In 1924, when she was eighteen, Lilly finally had enough money saved to pay for her trip to America.

When Lilly saw the Statue of Liberty, she felt she had finally achieved the first part of her dream. But after working for awhile in Philadelphia as a milliner, or hat-maker, Lilly was unhappy and thought of going back to France. One day she went into New York City on the train.

Suddenly, for the first time since she had come to America, Lilly saw skyscrapers and great stores and tall office buildings. Such excitement was going on, with hundreds of people creating sights and sounds around her. At that moment, Lilly knew she had found the America she was looking for.

Lilly Dache became a famous maker of ladies' hats. People from many countries ordered millinery from her. Through hard work and creative designing, Lilly became a success.

WHAT WOULD YOU DO?

Many people dreamed of America for years before they could come here. Lilly Dache was seven when she first wanted to leave France. Many problems were ahead of her.

1. If you were Lilly, and still in France, what could you do to prepare yourself for life in America?
2. What trades or professions would you suggest to young girls who wished to support themselves in a new land?
3. How could others learn a trade if they didn't speak English?

How were Swiss immigrants important?

Groups of Swiss immigrants who came to America settled mainly in the middle western states during the last half of the nineteenth century. Many of the Swiss people spoke a Swiss-German language and their habits and customs were very much like the Germans. The Swiss joined the Germans in singing and dramatic societies. They often became part of the German communities.

In their new country the Swiss often found the same kind of work they had done in Switzerland. Production of cheese in Wisconsin was started largely by the Swiss. Our watchmaking industry was built by the Swiss, also. Many of the Swiss became farmers. Swiss skill and training gave many good things to America.

There were many famous Swiss-Americans. Albert Gallatin came from a wealthy Swiss family. He wanted to live in America to work for his own future. He was active in government and became the Secretary of the Treasury for Presidents Jefferson and Madison. A tributary of the Missouri River was named for him.

Wisconsin was a favorite place for Swiss immigrants to begin farming.

In addition to his mill, John Sutter also built this fort. Within the settlement were a tannery, blanket factory, smithy, and other shops.

Captain John Sutter was another Swiss-American. He founded a settlement that later became Sacramento, California. It was here that the center of mining activities took place following the discovery of gold at Sutter's Mill in 1848.

Louis Agassiz (1807-1873) was a Swiss-American naturalist. He was famous for his work in zoology and geology. He started a summer school for science students on an island off the coast of Massachusetts. This was the first school for studying science in natural surroundings. It made the study of natural science much more real and interesting for students. Agassiz played a very important part in laying the foundation for the National Academy of Sciences, which does research and advises the government.

Some Swiss people found work in large cities in hotels and restaurants. Lorenzo Delmonico was a Swiss-American. He came to New York in 1832 and was known as America's teacher of good cooking and eating. The famous "Oscar of the Waldorf" was a well-known chef in the Waldorf Hotel in New York City. He was Oscar Tschirky, a Swiss immigrant.

"Oscar of the Waldorf" was a famous chef and host at this hotel.

WHAT WOULD YOU DO?

Suppose you were Oscar Tschirky, a chef who had just come from Switzerland to find a job in America. Think about how you would solve these problems.

1. Where might you begin looking for work?
2. How would you apply for a job if you had difficulty with the English language?
3. How could you get a restaurant owner to give you a chance to show what you can do?
4. As a chef, whom must you please other than your employer?
5. Why might you have left Switzerland to come to a new country?

Who were Dutch immigrants to America?

The Dutch were among the earliest settlers in the new world. Their numbers were small, but their influence was strong. The first settlers came to Manhattan Island in 1624. Two years later, New Amsterdam was established. It was the first permanent settlement on Manhattan. The Dutch were also living in the valley of the Hudson River. Peter Stuyvesant (1610-1672) was the last of the six governors of this area. He was a very stern and powerful governor, but in 1664 Stuyvesant was forced to surrender to the English. New Amsterdam became New York, but the Dutch influence remained. The Dutch language continued to be spoken. Along the banks of the Hudson River, the fine mansions built in the 1600's by Dutch landlords may still be seen. Names such as the Catskill Mountains and the Schuylkill River are Dutch.

The reasons for Dutch immigration to America in the nineteenth century were the same as they were for other early immigrant groups. Most people were looking for better jobs or were seeking religious freedom. Immigration offered a chance to escape the

Bowling "on the green" was a favorite outdoor sport with the Dutch who came to America. The game is somewhat like our modern version.

poverty that many people faced. Small Dutch farm colonies grew during the nineteenth century in Kansas, Nebraska, the Dakotas, Minnesota, and Illinois. Today, Dutch names can still be seen on shop signs and churches all over the United States.

By 1900 there were more than 105,000 Dutch-Americans who had been born in the Netherlands. Many of these people were living in Michigan, Illinois, and Iowa. During the next decade, more Dutch began arriving. Many of them stayed in Eastern cities.

As part of the festival in Michigan, townspeople clean the streets as in days of old.

The large Dutch settlement in Michigan has been very successful in farming. The May tulip festival in Holland, Michigan attracts visitors from all parts of the world.

Dutch-Americans have become prominent in many fields. Among them was Hendrik Van Loon (1882-1944), a historian and journalist. He was born in Rotterdam and came to the United States at the age of twenty. He won the Newberry Medal for his *History of Mankind*. The Van Doren brothers, Carl and Mark, each received a Pulitzer Prize for his writing.

There were three American presidents who came from Dutch backgrounds. These Presidents were Martin Van Buren, Theodore Roosevelt, and Franklin D. Roosevelt.

Edward Bok's Singing Tower was built to thank America for its help to immigrants.

Edward William Bok came to New York City from the Netherlands in 1870. He was only 7 years old. The young boy could not speak English. He had to leave school while very young. His family was poor, and Edward had to go to work. But he was determined to succeed. For many years, Edward went to night school after working all day. Soon success came. Edward Bok started his own newspaper when he was only 24. A short time later, he became editor of the famous "Ladies' Home Journal." Bok became well-known as an editor, journalist, reformer, and author. He won the Pulitzer Prize in 1921 for *The Americanization of Edward Bok.* Later he was known for his great gifts to the nation. One of the gifts was a beautiful park in Florida. Here stands one of the world's largest carillons, or bell towers. Carved on the tower are Bok's words thanking America for giving all immigrants a chance to build better lives for themselves.

WHAT WOULD YOU DO?

Imagine you are young Edward Bok. You have just learned that your family needs money. You have to leave school and find work.

1. Will you take the first job you can find or will you try to find work you like to do?
2. Why would you think it was important to go to school?
3. Why do you especially want to do well in your new country?

The design on this chest is an example of the decorative work done by the Pennsylvania Dutch.

What have Germans contributed to American life?

Large German settlements were built in New York State and in Pennsylvania. Many more Germans headed west where they could farm the land. Germans had a great love of the land. To some Americans, the Germans seemed to be "penny pinchers." This means they were very careful of every penny they spent. The German farmers prized their land. They saved money to buy farms.

Some of these farmers were called Pennsylvania Dutch. They were not Dutch at all. They were German. When English-speaking officials asked the German immigrants what language they spoke, they answered, "Deutsch." This means German. Through this mis-understanding, the Pennsylvania Germans came to be known as Pennsylvania Dutch. They were very good farmers. Their big, two-story barns were like the barns built in southern Germany. The Pennsylvania Dutch were very superstitious. They used hex signs on their houses and barns to chase away evil spirits. Some of these designs may still be seen on houses and barns in this region.

German immigration soon became greater than that of any other country. From 1820 to 1900, about five million Germans came to

The custom of decorating Christmas trees was brought to America by Germans.

the United States. The German immigrant did not look back and long to return to his native land. He planned to stay in America and give his best efforts to his new life in the new land.

Many German immigrants were well-trained and well-educated. During the early nineteenth century, American science was not as advanced as that of Europe. Germans helped lead the way to modern science in America. Many well-trained German doctors came to the United States as immigrants. They helped improve the training of new doctors in American medical schools and taught new ideas of medicine.

The Germans brought many holiday traditions with them. Christmas was always celebrated in a special way in Germany. New England Puritans did not celebrate Christmas in the happy way it is observed today. In time, Americans began to decorate evergreen trees and sing Christmas carols. These customs were part of the German culture.

German immigrants brought other customs which were new to Americans. They had concerts, card parties, and picnics on Sundays. They listened to band music in restaurant gardens. This kind of behavior was not well-liked in some American communities where Sunday was a day for going to church, not meant for fun. Later, American customs changed in many communities. Sunday became a day for family recreation as well as for church.

Most of the Germans in the city were skilled craftsmen, or people who work at trades. They helped American industries grow. In the cities, Germans processed food and made steel and pianos. They worked as printers, engineers, builders, and tradesmen.

In 1830 and 1848 there were revolutions in Germany. After that, many Germans in government and education came to the United States to find peace and freedom. Their knowledge added much to the fields of education, science, government, and arts.

The Germans had many other reasons for coming to America. The population was growing very fast, and Germany was becoming crowded. There were religious problems and wars. Crop failures brought hunger to many. Because of these problems some Germans looked for a new life in a new land. Their habits of hard work and their skills made them good citizens in the new land.

The Germans brought an interest in good music to the new land. They started symphony orchestras in most of the large cities. Leopold Damrosch (1832-1885) and his son Walter (1862-1950), helped build the famous New York Philharmonic Orchestra. At first,

Walter Damrosch conducts a rehearsal of the New York Philharmonic Orchestra.

Carl Schurz, lawyer and editor, believed firmly in German immigrants becoming a real part of American life.

the orchestra was made up entirely of German immigrants. Later other nationality groups became members. The Germans also started singing societies and glee clubs, groups of people who like to sing together. Attending singing society meetings brought German immigrants together for fun and music. Soon the idea of singing groups spread. Today many Americans take part in them.

Kindergarten was started from the German pre-school education. The name kindergarten is a German word meaning "children's garden." The Germans also began Turner Societies in the United States. These gymnastic groups helped people become physically fit. Today, German words and customs are still in use. Sausages and frankfurters are German foods enjoyed by almost everyone. German newspapers are still read, and many public schools teach German as a second language. In some American cities, the German people still live together in neighborhoods. They have kept many of their customs and traditions.

There were some fears that the German immigrants would stay together and form their own German state. Some German leaders, such as Carl Schurz, believed that the Germans should not stay apart from other Americans. Slowly the Germans became part of their new country.

Carl Schurz (1829-1906) came to America in 1848 for political freedom. He became a successful lawyer and editor. Because of his skill and service to his new country, Carl Schurz was made Ambassador to Spain. But he wanted to play a more active part in working for America. He gave up this job to enter the Union Army. He served in the Civil War and became a Major General. Later he served as a senator and as Secretary of the Interior.

Another famous German was John Augustus Roebling, a builder of bridges. He designed the first suspension bridge at Pittsburgh, Pennsylvania. Some other famous bridges constructed by Roebling were the Brooklyn Bridge and one at Niagara Falls, New York.

The field of science is filled with famous people of German background. Charles Steinmetz came to the United States in 1889. He became one of the world's greatest inventors. His work was in the field of electricity. Albert Michelson was a German-born physicist. He made important discoveries in the field of light and won the Nobel Prize for physics. For many years he headed the Department of Physics at the University of Chicago.

Charles Steinmetz overcame a lifelong handicap of being crippled. His work in mathematics, engineering, and electrical inventions gave him a firm place in history.

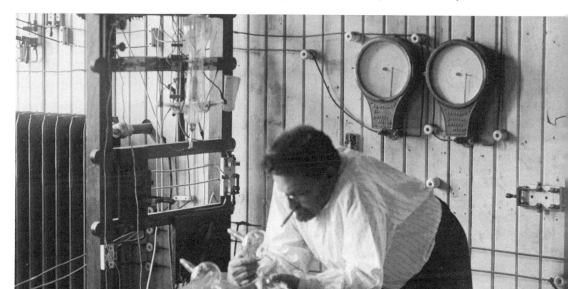

The knowledge of rocketry was helped in America by German scientists who came here during World War II.

The United States fought against Germany in World War I and World War II. These were difficult times for Germans who had come here as immigrants. Many Americans feared that the German-Americans might still be loyal to the old country. This was not true, and many, many German-Americans served in the American Army.

General John J. Pershing, a descendent of early German immigrants, was commander of the American forces in Europe in World War I. Another descendent of immigrant Germans was General Dwight Eisenhower. He was the commander of the American forces in Europe in World War II. In later years, he was elected our 34th president.

During World War II, many well-educated Germans left their homeland for America. They did not like the Nazi government, which was in power in Germany. The United States gained a great deal from the many outstanding Germans who came here to escape their government. Dr. Wernher Von Braun, a German-born scientist, brought America his great knowledge of missiles and rockets. He helped build the American space program. In 1958 Dr. Von Braun became an American citizen.

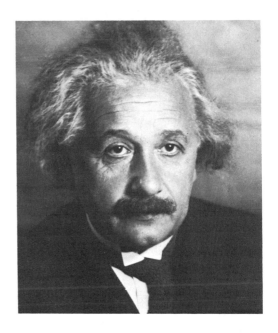

Albert Einstein was a genius in math and science. Your library may have interesting books about him for you to read.

The most famous scientist to come to America from Germany was Albert Einstein (1879-1955). His most talked about theory, or idea, changed the scientific views of time, space, and motion.

While Einstein was visiting the United States in 1933, the German government took away his job, property, and citizenship. He then stayed in America as a director of mathematics in Princeton, New Jersey. He became a citizen in 1940 and lived here until his death. Although he is remembered for his scientific genius, he also worked hard for world peace.

WHAT WOULD YOU DO?

Suppose you were Albert Einstein. You are speaking to a group of world leaders about the need for controlling nuclear power.

1. What could you say to help them understand the need to stop the race for nuclear power?
2. Why must peaceful uses of nuclear energy be used rather than destructive uses?
3. Why would your words as Albert Einstein carry great importance in a conference with world leaders?
4. What might you as Einstein say to a group of students to get their support for peaceful solutions to world problems?

Norwegians of long ago stored food in "stabburs," away from animals.

What have the Scandinavians contributed to American life?

Scandinavians were among the first explorers of the new world. Some historians believe that Leif Ericson discovered America long before the voyage of Christopher Columbus. However, no permanent Scandinavian settlement was made in the new world until 1638. At that time, about fifty Swedes, under the leadership of Frenchman Peter Minuit, built a Swedish colony along the Delaware River. Minuit had been dismissed earlier by the Dutch as director-general of the New Netherlands colony. He went to Sweden and got permission to establish a Swedish colony. A fort was built at what is now Wilmington, Delaware. It was called New Sweden. In 1658 the Dutch, under Peter Stuyvesant, seized the Swedish fort. Later the British took the land away from the Dutch.

It was not until the 1840's that the number of Scandinavians began to increase in the United States. The Scandinavian countries include Sweden, Norway, Iceland, Finland, and Denmark. Between the Civil War and World War II, more than one million Swedes came to America. Norwegian immigration reached its peak in 1882. At that time, about 30,000 arrived. Many Norwegians settled in Minnesota, Wisconsin, and Illinois. Some settled in Washington and Oregon, as well as in New York.

The Danes also began arriving in large numbers in the middle of the nineteenth century. The largest number of Danes arrived in

America in 1881-1890. About 88,000 came at that time. People from Finland came and settled in Michigan and Massachusetts. The wave of Scandinavian immigration ended in the 1930's. It is said that in the United States today there are ten million Americans of Scandinavian birth or descent.

The Scandinavians had a busy life in the old country. Now on the frontier they cut down trees, built their homes, and prepared the land for farming. Some became loggers in the Pacific Northwest. They cut the trees for lumber. Their outdoor experience in their native lands helped prepare them for this rugged life.

The people from Denmark who settled the rural areas knew all about dairy farming. They produced milk and other dairy products, such as cheese and butter. They helped make cheese a very important product in America.

The Scandinavian people had been in great need of land. There was little land for them to buy in their own countries. Many people then left their homelands to go to America. They hoped to buy

Norwegians brought the idea of sod roofs to America. Animals grazed on the grass.

land in America and start their own farms. Officials in Scandinavian countries worried that they would lose too many of their hard-working people to the new land.

Getting started in the new land was not easy for the newcomers. The men in the family worked as farmhands or construction workers for one dollar a day. The women became maids. But within a few years, many families began buying land to farm. Land could be bought from the government at a very low price. Many Scandinavian immigrants came to America in groups and settled together in a community. Here their holiday and religious customs could be carried on quite easily.

The Scandinavians helped public education in many ways. They began adult education programs and 4-H clubs. Colleges were founded by both the Norwegians and the Swedes. Among them are Augustana College, St. Olaf College, and Upsala College. The immigrants of the Scandinavian countries added to American life through their choral groups, journalists, artists, and scientists.

Not all immigrants who came to America were poor. This wealthy Swedish family came to America in 1879.

The Scandinavians are a warm and friendly people. They have deep feelings for their home and family. Their holiday customs, their love of good food, and their artistic decorations are still enjoyed in this country. Swedish clubs and restaurants serve smor-gasbord, a meal with many, many kinds of food. The traditional Swedish Lucia Festival is also enjoyed each year by the many families of Swedish descent.

This girl is dressed in a traditional Scandinavian costume.

Who were some famous Scandinavian immigrants?

A Swedish immigrant, John Ericson (1803-1889), planned and drew the famous propeller-driven warship, the *Monitor*. This great warship was very important in the Civil War and in naval history. Ericsson also built canal boats, ships, and merchant steamers.

Knute Rockne was born in Norway. He became a famous football player and coach at the University of Notre Dame. Rockne was considered one of the greatest coaches in football.

Dr. Ernst F. W. Alexanderson was born in Sweden and came to the United States in 1901. He was a famous inventor in electrical and mechanical engineering. One of his inventions helped perfect the guiding system for aircraft. One of the best-known inventors of Scandinavian descent was the Swede, Vincent Bendix. He Invented the self-starter for cars. He also developed the Bendix Aviation Corporation and Bendix Helicopters, Inc.

Charles A. Lindbergh, Sr., came to America from Sweden when he was very young. Lindbergh became a lawyer and a well-known Congressman from Minnesota. His son, Charles Lindbergh, Jr., flew the first nonstop flight across the ocean to Paris in 1927.

Ole Rolvaag came to the United States when he was twenty years old. In Norway he had been a fisherman, but he wanted to build a new life in America. He came to America in 1896 and worked on farms for some years. After he had saved some money, he began to put himself through school. Later he entered college and became a professor at St. Olaf College. Rolvaag became famous for his books about Norwegian immigrants, especially *Giants in the Earth*.

The Scandinavian-Americans were known for their hard work, thrift, honesty, pride in home, and respect for education. All of these qualities helped them build fine communities. These immigrant groups enriched America in many different ways.

Scandinavians took great pride in homemaking. The plates on the mantel are decorated with Norwegian Rosemaling, or rose painting, a favorite Norwegian folk art.

Jacob August Riis came to America from Denmark when he was twenty-one years old. For three years he worked at many different jobs. Riis had a hard time those first years in his new country. Then he began to work as a newspaper reporter. He was very concerned about conditions in New York's slums. Soon he began to take pictures and write articles that told about the bad conditions in the slums. His book, called *How the Other Half Lives*, made him well-known. Through his writing and work, he helped bring changes to New York's slums. Jacob Riis became famous as a great reformer who worked all his life to help the poor people of his new country.

WHAT WOULD YOU DO?

Suppose you were Jacob Riis, writer and reporter, living in New York City. What would you do about the problems you see in the city's slums?

1. What kind of social problems might you find in an inner-city slum neighborhood?
2. How could you get people interested in helping improve the housing, education, and recreation in these neighborhoods?
3. What might you say in a speech to a group of citizens about the need to improve housing and education?
4. Who would pay for these improvements?
5. Do you think the problems of slum areas are different today from those of one hundred years ago when Jacob Riis first came to the United States?

WHAT DO YOU THINK?

1. What are some of the Northern and Western European countries from which immigrants came?
2. How did the immigration movement help the United States?
3. Did it hurt the United States to have so many poor people coming here to find work? Why or why not?
4. Why were singing societies and clubs popular with early immigrants such as the Germans and Scandinavians?

5. What added problems did the French and German immigrants have that were not faced by the English immigrants?
6. How did professionally trained immigrants in science and medicine help the United States? Why did these successful people want to leave their homeland?
7. Why did more German immigrants, rather than other groups, settle on farms?
8. Do you think there were more opportunities for people to get good jobs in the 1880's than there are today? Why?

9. Why were the unskilled workers, as well as the skilled workers, important to the development of the United States?
10. Are there food shortages and crop failures anywhere in the world today? Where?
11. How does the large food supply of the United States help these underfed people?
12. How did the immigrants of Northern and Western Europe help build the United States? How did the United States help them?

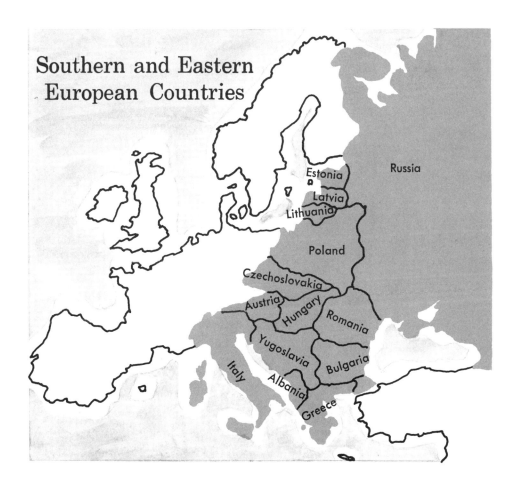

Southern and Eastern European Countries

Immigration from Southern and Eastern Europe

Immigration to America changed in about 1900. At this time most of the new immigrants came from southern and eastern Europe. They came from such countries as Italy, Greece, Albania, Bulgaria, Romania, Yugoslavia, Austria, Hungary, Poland, Russia, and what is now Czechoslovakia. These immigrants, like others, came to America to find a better life in a new country.

The new immigrants were very poor and had little education. Their problems were even greater than those of the earlier immigrants. They had trouble learning the new language and customs. The religion of most of the new immigrants was Greek Orthodox or Roman Catholic. Most Americans were Protestant. These new and different religious groups were not always welcomed by the Americans who had been here longer.

Most of the new immigrants came from farms and small villages. Many of them had to settle in the cities where they could find work and earn money quickly. They usually lived near the center of the city or business district where the buildings were old and crowded. Slums grew out of some of these neighborhoods. When the older immigrants made enough money, they usually moved out to the newer and better parts of the city. As other immigrants came, they moved into the center of the city, left empty by the old immigrants. Some neighborhoods were first English, then German, then Irish, then Polish, and then Negro areas in the center of the cities.

Courtesy Chicago Historical Society

Today new groups are still moving into the old immigrant neighborhoods in big cities. They are mostly black and Hispano American peoples. The old areas have poor housing and social problems. Big cities are working hard on urban renewal to help improve these neighborhoods. Many of the buildings now being torn down were the first homes of the early immigrants

This picture shows a street scene in one of the immigrant neighborhoods around the turn of the century.

This Italian family is waiting on Ellis Island. This picture was drawn about 1900.

How did the Italians help America?

Italians were among the early explorers of the new world. Christopher Columbus was an Italian. Amerigo Vespucci was another Italian explorer. His writings about the New World led a map-maker to use the name Amerigo to refer to the new continents of North and South America. Italian missionaries and some early settlers came to America during the 18th century. Many Italians served in America's Civil War in 1865.

It was the beginning of the 20th century before large numbers of Italian immigrants came to America. Many people were leaving the southern part of Italy because of poverty. The farmland in Italy was poor and Italian farmers were having hard times. In America, industry was developing rapidly. New factories and mills were being built in every big American city. More manpower was needed. The Italians came to fill this need for labor. More than five million Italians came to the United States between 1890 and 1963. They became the second-largest national group of immigrants here. Only the German-Americans outnumbered them.

Most of these Italian immigrants were very poor and had little education. They found work in the cities along the Northeastern seaboard. A few were able to find agricultural jobs. Some traveled to California to work in the vineyards, where grapes were grown. The cost of land was too high for most of these people to buy their own farms.

Many of the early immigrants planned to stay in the United States long enough to save some money and then return home. Often the men would come to the United States and leave their families in Italy. They would return to Italy later with their savings. However, the time soon came when many Italians began to think of America as their new, permanent home. Some urban areas in America had nearly all Italians living in them. These neighborhoods were known as "Little Italy." Most large cities had an Italian section. Mulberry Street on the Lower East Side of New York City was one such "Little Italy." In the 1880's Mulberry Street seemed to be a little world in itself. It had Italian stores, small restaurants, bakeries, and newspapers. It also had boarding houses for the newest immigrants.

Children of immigrants in New York had very little space to play. Here they try to cool off on a hot summer day.

As time went by, the Italian immigrants and their children improved their lives. They moved from the lowest jobs to some of the best ones.

The Italian immigrants in the big cities usually became laborers. They helped build subways, cleaned streets, and worked in the stockyards or in the mills. As had other immigrants before them, the Italians moved upward from less skilled jobs to the more skilled trades. Thousands joined the building-trade unions. They became carpenters, electricians, and plumbers. Some became the owners of small businesses. Others were barbers and tailors. Many Italian women did sewing to add to the family income.

Italian families were often large. They were very close and loyal to each other. With hard work and courage the Italians became good American citizens. They kept their loyalty and strong ties to their family and church. Because of this they built a better life for themselves and also helped America grow greater. Second- and third-generation Italians have entered and become well-known in all the professions. They remain proud of their Italian heritage.

Constantino Brumidi spent almost thirty years painting the famous murals in the Capitol Building in Washington, D.C.

Who are some famous Italian-American immigrants?

One of the men who helped open up the Northwest Territory was an Italian, Colonel Francis Vigo (1747-1836). Colonel Vigo helped General George Rogers Clark capture Fort Vincennes from the British in 1779. This victory is thought to have opened the West for the United States.

One of the greatest women to come to the United States from Italy was Mother Frances Cabrini. She was the founder of the Order of the Missionary Sisters of the Sacred Heart. She came in 1889 to work with needy Italians. She opened an orphanage for Italian children in New York City. Later she added a church and hospital. Mother Cabrini worked in many other cities throughout the United States. After her death she was declared a saint. She was the first American to be given this special honor by the Roman Catholic Church.

Italians have always been producers and lovers of fine art. Constantino Brumidi (1805-1880) was a famous painter. He painted the historical murals in the rotunda and dome of the Capitol in Washington, D.C. This great work took him almost thirty years. Attilio Piccirilli was a sculptor. His *Maine Memorial* was erected in New York City in memory of the servicemen of the Spanish-American war. A modern artist is Antonio Salemme. His bronze head of the late President Eisenhower is very famous.

One of Mario Lanza's many title roles was in "Pagliacci." It is a great Italian opera.

The musical talents of the Italian-American were many. In 1883 when the New York Metropolitan Opera House was opened, an Italian was one of the first conductors. This was Cleofante Campanini. In Chicago he later became both conductor and manager of the Opera Association. Arturo Toscanini (1867-1952) was a famous Italian immigrant. He was one of the great musical conductors of the New York Philharmonic Orchestra.

Enrico Caruso (1873-1921) was born in Naples. He became famous as a grand opera tenor at the age of twenty-one. He starred in the Metropolitan Opera from 1903-1920. Giovanni Martinelli was his successor in that opera house. A third well-loved Italian tenor was Mario Lanza (1921-1959). He carried on the great songs that Caruso made famous, but preferred movies to the stage. One of his finest films was the biography, "The Great Caruso." Through the years thousands of Americans enjoyed hearing these singers.

There are many success stories about poor Italians who became millionaires. Amadeo Giannini was the son of immigrants. He began working for a produce company at the age of twelve. As a young man he opened a small bank in San Francisco which he called the Bank of Italy. It is now the Bank of America, the largest in the United States. Other big businesses, such as the La Rosa Macaroni Company, were built by successful Italian immigrants.

Joe DiMaggio was a foremost outfielder and is very well-known. He is still active in the world of baseball.

One of the best-known Italian-Americans was the man Fiorello LaGuardia (1882-1947). He was born in America of Italian-born parents. When LaGuardia was a young man he worked as a lawyer to help garment workers during the strikes. He helped new immigrants by serving as interpreter on Ellis Island. La Guardia became active in politics and later became mayor of New York City. His love of people and his fight against discrimination and corruption made him an outstanding and popular public figure.

The field of sports is one in which Italian-Americans have excelled. Many sports, especially boxing and baseball, have produced outstanding athletes. Rocky Marciano gained fame as the world champion heavyweight boxer, while Rocky Graziano claimed the championship in the middleweight division. In baseball there have been many famous Italian-American stars. Joe DiMaggio of the New York Yankees was one of baseball's greatest stars and is a member of the National Baseball Hall of Fame. Among the other famous baseball stars are many great names such as Phil Rizzuto, Gino Cimoli, and Joe Garagiola.

Mr. Garagiola has also become well-known as a television entertainer. Other well-known names in the entertainment world are those of Perry Como, Frank Sinatra, and Dean Martin, all of whom are of Italian descent.

One immigrant lived his childhood in poverty and went on to help others who came to live in America. Edward Corsi was born in Italy and came to America in 1907 as a young boy. He and his parents, brother, and sisters lived in a tenement on the East Side of New York City. They were very poor and sometimes had no food in their apartment. Edward was disappointed in America. He had heard such wonderful stories about it while he was still in Italy. But to the young immigrant boy in New York, America did not seem to be such a wonderful place.

When he was a teenager, Edward discovered a settlement house in his neighborhood. This changed his life. He became interested in helping younger boys organize teams of various kinds. He worked to help solve neighborhood problems. This work helped him learn of and love the promise of America.

When Edward graduated from college, he was made director of that same settlement house, by then called Haarlem House. He went on to become Commissioner of Immigration at Ellis Island, where he could help others as he himself had once needed help.

WHAT WOULD YOU DO?

Edward Corsi chose to spend his life helping immigrants in America. Imagine yourself in his job.

1. Why would you choose this job rather than another?
2. In what ways would you try to help people who are new to the United States?
3. In your job as Commissioner of Immigration, you help others every day. What could you do in your old neighborhood to help there also?

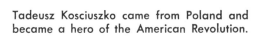
Tadeusz Kosciuszko came from Poland and became a hero of the American Revolution.

How have the Polish people helped America?

The date when the first Poles arrived in America is not known. Some historians think that explorers who lived in what later became Poland may have sailed with Columbus. Some Poles immigrated to America in the colonial times. Some came as indentured servants to the Southern colonies.

During the Revolutionary War, the many Americans of Polish descent fought bravely in the struggle for independence from Britain. They were joined by two famous men who came all the way from Poland to help the Americans in their fight for freedom.

Tadeusz Kosciuszko (1746-1817) and Casimir Pulaski (1748-1779) were those two soldiers. Neither one became an American citizen. But they came from Poland to help in the fight for the liberty of our new nation. Kosciuszko had studied engineering in France. He was appointed colonel of engineers in the Continental Army. After Pulaski met Benjamin Franklin in France, he came to America and served in General Washington's army. He was made Chief of Cavalry by the Congress.

In 1800 the Polish population in the United States was quite small. Several hundred more Poles came to America as refugees shortly after 1830. This was a time of uprisings in Poland when many wished to escape to a land where there was more freedom.

These immigrants arrived at Ellis Island in 1912, to be admitted to the United States. Much of their lives ahead was uncertain.

The largest number of Poles began to arrive in the 1870's. The high point of Polish immigration came just before World War I. Nearly 175,000 Polish people entered America in one year.

Poles coming to America wanted better jobs. Polish farm villages were very poor and crowded. The Polish immigrants who came to the United States were mostly peasants looking for a better life. Few had a trade or much education. But they were willing to work hard and save their money to buy homes.

Polish farming communities grew in Massachusetts, New York, Ohio, Indiana, Illinois, and Texas. But most Poles lived in cities where they worked as laborers. Poles replaced the Irish in textile mills, packing houses, stockyards, and mines.

The Poles organized into hundreds of societies. The largest and oldest is the Polish National Alliance. Its purpose once was the

These people in costume are enjoying a parade in honor of their native Poland.

moral and material improvement of Polish immigrants. The Polish National Alliance continues to serve its people long after the period of mass Polish immigration.

The customs of the Polish immigrants seemed strange to some Americans. Poles were not accepted in many communities. As had other immigrant groups, they found they enjoyed life more if they lived near each other and shared their Polish customs.

The Roman Catholic Church has always been important in the Polish-American community. However, there were Polish Jews and Protestants among the newcomers. Churches served as social agencies for the immigrants. They were an important part of social and religious life and a means of the children's education.

Gradually these immigrants became better educated. In the second and third generations professional men began to appear among them. Many Polish people had an influence on America. Polish traditions have been kept alive through many organizations and through family customs. The festivals, parades, and celebrations help Americans remember that our country has benefited greatly from the hard work and talent of the Polish people.

In some cities there are special Polish schools which meet on Saturdays. Here the students learn the language and the history of Poland. In Chicago alone there are twelve of these schools. There are also many Polish folk dance groups, Scout troops, and summer camps which help teach the culture and traditions of Poland to the children of Polish immigrants.

North of Poland, bordering the Baltic Sea, are the three small countries of Lithuania, Latvia, and Estonia. Because of their locations, they are known as the Baltic countries. These lands have had a history of being ruled by other nations. Russia and Germany have been the major ruling powers. In 1944, near the close of the Second World War, Russia gained power over the small Baltic nations. Since that time the three countries have become states in the Soviet Union.

America has welcomed immigrants from these countries. They love the freedom and security which they have found here in their new land. While they have become good Americans, they also have remembered and taught their children the language and customs of their native homelands.

These Lithuanian-Americans are doing one of their national dances. They are dressed in costumes that are native to Lithuania.

Helena Modjeska was well-known in her native land. She also became famous in America.

Who are some well-known Poles?

There are many Polish-Americans in politics and government. One of the best-known is Edmund Muskie, who became the governor of Maine and later a United States senator. He was a candidate for vice-president in 1968 and is still active in government.

Helena Modjeska (1840-1909) was born in Poland. She came to America in 1876. She worked hard to learn English so she could continue her acting career here. She became successful and made tours around the country. Helena played many parts, including Shakespearian characters, in both English and Polish.

In the world of music, some well-known Poles have been Leopold Stokowski, Artur Rodzinski, and Wanda Landowska, the harpsichordist. There have been fine athletes of Polish ancestry in many different sports. Two of the best known names in baseball are Stan Musial and Carl Yastrzemski.

Casimir Funk (1884-1967) was a famous biochemist. He discovered that some diseases are caused by a lack of certain substances, or chemicals, in food. These substances he named vitamines. The name was later changed to vitamins. Another scientist, this one a physicist, is Emil Konopinski. He played a very important part in the development of the atomic bomb.

One of Modjeski's best-known bridges is one between San Francisco and Oakland, California. It was built in 1936 and is more than eight miles long.

Ralph Modjeski was the son of actress Helena Modjeska. He was born in Cracow, Poland, in 1861, and studied in Paris to become an engineer. When he finished school in France, Modjeski came to America. In the growing nation he became well-known as a designer and builder of great bridges. Modjeski helped build many of the new bridges in the United States which have, in turn, helped millions of people in this country.

WHAT WOULD YOU DO?

Imagine that you are young Ralph Modjeski in Paris. You want to become a great engineer. What would you do?

1. Why might you go to America to become an engineer?
2. You are a young man just out of school and an immigrant in a new country. How would you find your first job?
3. Do you think your Polish nationality will help or hurt you?

How have the Czechs helped America?

The word Czech refers to the people and language found in Bohemia and Moravia. Slovak is the name given to the eastern groups of the Czech-speaking people. The Slovak language is similar to the Czech language.

Czechs settled in America as early as the colonial period. Their number was small until the 1840's. Then the potato famine swept Bohemia, causing more people to leave. The number of Czechs in America increased until 1870, then slowed down until about 1890. From then until 1914 thousands more Czechs came here. Slovak immigration to the United States began about 1873. By 1920 there were 400,000 Slovaks in the United States. Poverty and the wish for political freedom were the main reasons for these people coming to America.

Large Czech farm settlements began to grow in Iowa, Wisconsin, Nebraska, Kansas, Oklahoma, and Texas. By 1910 there were over 500,000 foreign-born persons of Bohemian and Moravian background in America. Most of these immigrants lived in the Midwest. Chicago eventually became one of the largest Czech settlements in the United States. Neighborhoods reflected the old world Czech culture. There were foreign newspapers, Czech theaters, butcher shops with homemade sausage, bakeries with old world pastries, and restaurants which specialized in Czech food.

This traditional European-style design is on a popular Czech restaurant near Chicago.

This factory in Pennsylvania employed many people. It is one of those that hired immigrants in the early part of the 20th century.

The Czech immigrants did not usually work at unskilled outdoor jobs. They worked in factories and shops. Many Czechs were musicians and tailors. There were few professionally-trained Czechs among the early immigrants. However, within a generation the number of Czech lawyers, doctors, and politicians grew.

Many of the Slovaks went to the mining and industrial centers of the United States for jobs. Large numbers of the immigrants from this group could not read. They scattered throughout the United States. The largest settlement was in Pennsylvania because the heavy industries there offered jobs. A few of the Slovak immigrant families went into farming in New England.

In 1918 the Czech and Slovak peoples were united in Europe to form Czechoslovakia. The new country joined what were once Bohemia and Moravia. Although the two peoples were united in Europe, in America they remained separate groups.

In 1948 the Communists overthrew the Czechoslovakian democratic government. This caused another wave of Czech immigrants to come to America. About 30,000 newcomers came seeking political freedom. Many of these people were well-educated and professional people. They were different from the early immigrants, who had had little education or training.

The Czechs enjoyed being active in Sokol, a gymnastic group. Sokol is famous for its work in physical fitness. There were groups here and in Europe. The Czech immigrants helped start even more Sokol programs in the United States. Many Sokol groups are still active today and used by Americans of all backgrounds.

In the field of music the Czechs also made great contributions. During the Civil War there were many Czech musicians. Czechs were bandmasters for West Point and in army and navy posts. Anton Dvorak was a famous composer. He worked in America and wrote his famous New World Symphony while visiting in Spillville, a small Czech settlement in Iowa. Later he returned to Europe, where he died in 1904. Dvorak did not become an American citizen, but he had great influence in the writing of both American and Slovak national music.

Physical fitness is important to good health. These children are enjoying their playground activity.

Rudolf Friml was another well-known Czech musician. He was a concert pianist and a composer of semi-classical music and light opera. Friml made a concert tour of the United States in 1906 and decided to remain here. At one time he worked with Victor Herbert, the Irish composer. Today, Rudolf Serkin is a popular and highly respected concert pianist. This Czech-American has became famous for the beautiful music he presents to audiences.

One of many musicians of Czech descent, Rudolf Serkin has delighted countless people with his piano-playing.

In the field of science Czechs have also become well-known. Dr. Frederick Novy was one of America's greatest bacteriologists and Dr. Ales Hrdlicka became a famous anthropologist. Talented Czechs made their marks in American universities. Dr. John Zeleny was a noted physicist at the University of Minnesota, while Dr. Alois Kovarik worked at Yale.

World War II caused great hardship in Czechoslovakia. Many Czechs were forced to leave their homeland. America gained many talented Czech-American citizens. Zdenek Kopal came from Czechoslovakia to do important work in astronomy. George Placzek was a physicist who worked on American atomic projects.

In America today the arts, sciences, business, and government all have many Czech-American leaders whose ties go back one or more generations to their Czech ancestors.

This statue, in honor of Tomas Masa-ryk and Anton Cermak, also honors all Czechoslovakian Americans.

Anton Cermak was born in 1873 in Kladno, Czechoslovakia. When Cermak's family came to America, they settled in the city of Chicago. Here Anton Cermak became active in Chicago's politics and was elected mayor of Chicago in 1931. Cermak was considered a reform mayor. He worked hard to improve the big city. In 1933 a man tried to shoot President Franklin D. Roosevelt at a meeting in Florida. But Mayor Cermak was killed instead.

As a memorial to Anton Cermak, Chicagoans set up a monument. It is a statue of a crusader of old and is dedicated to Tomas Masaryk, a famous Czech. It was made by Albin Polasek, a Czech immigrant. The statue reads, in part: "Dedicated to Tomas Garrigue Masaryk, Crusader for Truth, Teacher, Liberator, Statesman."

WHAT WOULD YOU DO?

Suppose you are Anton Cermak, age 20. As a Czech-American in Chicago, you are active in the politics of the big city.

1. Why do you think you would choose to work so hard in the field of politics?
2. Why would your freedom to work for your beliefs mean so much to you, especially?
3. As a new American immigrant, what would be your feelings about how to run a city's government?

How have Russian immigrants contributed to America?

Russian fur traders came to North America as early as 1747. But there was not really much Russian immigration until about 1900. Then Russian immigration increased until World War I.

In 1917 the poor living and working conditions within Russia brought about the Russian Revolution. A communistic government took the place of rule by the czar. The new government brought many changes. Because of the revolution and the changes in Russia, many Russians left their homes and came to America at this time. Russian immigration ended soon after the revolution. The new government would not let Russians leave their country.

Many of the Russian immigrants were among the least-educated and poorest of all the newcomers. These people arrived in New York with no money. They had to work at the most unskilled jobs for the lowest pay. Some Russians went to work in the coal and steel areas. Many worked in lumber and fishing jobs. Others went to the fruit-growing regions of California. Russian immigrants did

Many Russians came to America as a result of the 1917 revolution in their home country. Coal-mining was one of the many jobs they had in America.

Joseph Stalin's daughter, Svetlana Alliluyeva, preferred America to her native Russia.

Igor Stravinsky became famous in 1910 when his ballet, The Firebird, was performed in Paris. He came to America in 1939.

not organize into groups or societies as much as other immigrant groups. Because they lacked trade skills, few Russians joined the craft unions. In later years some joined such unions as the United Mine Workers.

The Russian immigrants worked hard in their new world to make homes for themselves. Russian-Americans are now well-known in many areas of American life.

Several famous musicians and composers who came from Russia added much to American culture. Some of these great musicians are Mischa Elman, Jascha Heifetz, Igor Stravinsky, Vladimir Horowitz, and Nathan Milstein.

In 1967 the daughter of Joseph Stalin, a past leader of the Russian government, escaped from Russia and came to America. Svetlana Alliluyeva told the story of her life in Russia and her reasons for leaving that country in the book, Only One Year. Svetlana Alliluyeva had to escape from Russia because the government there still would not allow its people to leave freely.

Igor Sikorsky was one of the true pioneers in aviation. He was born in Kiev, Russia, in 1889. For many years Sikorsky studied in Russia and in Paris. He was always interested in mechanical things. As he grew older, he became most interested in aircraft and flight. He experimented a great deal with building airplanes. In 1919 Sikorsky left Paris and came to America. He had only a few hundred dollars when he arrived in the United States. At first he worked in a settlement house on New York's East Side. In 1923 some friends helped him begin work on his own airplane. After some disappointments, he finally produced a plane which was able to carry fourteen people. Later, Sikorsky built many new kinds of airplanes, such as the tri-motor, the amphibian, and the helicopter. He founded an aircraft company which later became part of the United Aircraft Corporation. This company produced many planes which were used by the military and by commercial airlines. Igor Sikorsky became a United States citizen in 1928.

WHAT WOULD YOU DO?

You are Igor Sikorsky, a young Russian in Paris. Your future is ahead of you. Will you choose to return to Russia or to go to live in a strange, new country? Consider some of the things you must think about before you make your decision.

1. You have spent many years of study in your field. You want to use your learning. Where will you be most able to experiment with aircraft and flight?
2. It is 1919. Are there any other countries in Europe where you can live in peace, security, and freedom? Why or why not?
3. You love your homeland of Russia. What are some of the many things that might make you decide you cannot return to your native country now?

These children in Greek costumes are parading during the anniversary of Greek independence.

What have the Greeks contributed to America?

The largest number of Greek immigrants came to America in the early 20th century. Before the start of World War II, about one-half million Greeks entered the United States. Under the quota laws passed after World War II, only about 300 Greek immigrants were permitted to enter the country yearly. However, many more came as refugees and students and remained here.

The Greek people came to America to earn a better living and improve their lives. At this time there was a great deal of poverty in the small Greek villages where the immigrants had lived . The early immigrants were mostly men who planned to return to Greece with money for their families. Many of the Greek people had been fishermen and shepherds. They were not prepared for the kind of jobs to be had in America.

The Greeks settled mostly in large cities. Many Greeks began life in America as street vendors and peddlers of fruit and vegetables. Some found jobs in the New England textile centers.

Although many Greek Orthodox churches are very old in design, the one shown here is modern.

Others worked in restaurants, on construction jobs, and in shoeshine parlors. They were very hard workers.

The Greek immigrants usually built a Greek Orthodox Church in their communities as soon as possible. There are about three hundred of these churches in America today. Greek schools, coffee houses, and clubs also became part of the immigrant neighborhoods. Today the Greek people are proud of their traditions and heritage and they work hard to preserve them.

Many Greeks have become very sucessful in businesses such as restaurants, floral shops, and candy stores. Greek-Americans have entered the professions, also. Dimitri Mitropoulos was the director of the New York Philharmonic Symphony Orchestra and conductor of the Metropolitan Opera. He was born in Athens. George Papanicolaou was a famous specialist in cancer research at Cornell University. He is credited with saving countless lives. Elia Kazan is well-known as a writer and movie director. One of the most famous Greek-Americans is Spiro Agnew, Vice-President of the United States under President Richard M. Nixon.

The three Skouras brothers, all born in Greece, are well-known in the entertainment world. As young men they worked hard to save enough money to buy one of the early moviehouses. Because theater owners at that time did not keep their buildings clean and pleasant, not many people went to the movies. The Skouras greatly improved their theater. Soon the new business was doing very well. Now there are more than one thousand theaters in the Skouras chain in America and around the world. One brother, Spyros, became president of the 20th Century Fox movie studio.

WHAT WOULD YOU DO?

The Skouras brothers were poor and unknown when they arrived in America. They worked together as a team to achieve their success. Imagine that you are one of them.

1. Would you mind doing unskilled jobs, living simply, and saving most of your money to achieve your dream?
2. When you bought your first theater, how would you improve it and give good service to movie-goers?
3. As a successful businessman, how would you show your gratitude to your new country?

The Pulitzer Prize was started by Joseph Pulitzer, an immigrant from Hungary. It is awarded to the journalist or newspaper that has done the greatest public service during that year.

What have Hungarians and Austrians contributed to America?

Hungarian immigrants first began to come to America in large numbers in about 1848. Many people left Hungary during the revolution against the Hungarian government.

Some Hungarians settled in farm communities of the United States. But most of them lived in the cities. They worked as laborers in factories and mines. Some were tailors, storekeepers, and restaurant owners. Hungarian communities grew in big cities such as New York, Cleveland, Chicago, and Detroit.

Edward Teller came to the United States from Hungary in 1940. He worked with the Atomic Energy Commission, then became a professor of physics at the University of California. He is known for his work in nuclear physics. Joseph Pulitzer came to New York without money or friends. He became known for his work and success in journalism. The Columbia School of Journalism was started with money given by Mr. Pulitzer. Each year Pulitzer Prize medals are given to the best writers in different fields.

Austria has given America many gifted people in the arts, law, and business. To escape the war in Europe, one of our well-known writers, Franz Werfel, came to America in 1940. His best-known book is *Song of Bernadette*. It was also a popular movie.

What have the people of the Balkan States contributed to America?

Albania, Bulgaria, Romania, and Yugoslavia are called the Balkan States because these nations are near the Balkan Mountains. The small Balkan countries have had a long history of war.

Over 300,000 immigrants have come to America from the Balkans, mostly during the 20th century. They worked hard in their new country to create good lives. Large cities attracted these people because there were jobs available. Some people found work in Pennsylvania and West Virginia in the coal and metal industries. Many Balkan people belonged to groups for gymnastics, singing, drama, or dancing. These groups helped preserve the customs and the traditions of the Balkan peoples.

Three of the most honored Balkan people who came to America were Nikola Tesla (1856-1943), Dr. Michael Pupin (1858-1935), and Louis Adamic (1899-1951). Tesla invented many electrical devices. Pupin worked in the fields of telephone, telegraph, and radio. Adamic wrote about immigrants in the United States. One of his well-known books is *The Native's Return*. A recent immigrant, born in Yugoslavia, is Dragos D. Kostich. He came to America in 1952 after graduating from the University of Paris. He has been a teacher of world affairs and has worked for Voice of America radio, making broadcasts to his native land.

These two immigrants from Romania were sketched at Ellis Island.

WHAT DO YOU THINK?

1. What are some of the Southern and Eastern European countries from which immigrants came to America?

2. Do you think some immigrants were disappointed when they discovered that life was not always easy in America? Explain.

3. How did some of the Southern and Eastern European immigrants contribute to new food habits of Americans?

4. How did the Southern and Eastern Europeans contribute to the advancement of music in America?

5. Do big cities still have "Little Italy" types of communities? Explain your feelings.

6. How are these neighborhoods changing?

7. How were the problems of the immigrants from Southern and Eastern Europe the same as the problems of the immigrants from Northern and Western Europe? How were they different?

8. Why were the immigrants from Southern and Eastern Europe not always welcomed by Americans? Was this in keeping with our democratic principles? Why?

9. When immigrants from Southern and Eastern Europe come to America today, what new problems do they face?

10. Why did the quota laws seem especially unfair to the Southern and Eastern European immigrants?

11. In Chapter Two you learned that the immigration laws of 1965 ended all quotas. How could this help the Southern and Eastern European immigrants?

The Spanish and the French explorers often had Negroes on their crews. They helped explore and build America.

The Negro Helped Build America

Negroes were among the first people to set foot in America. It is said that Pedro Alonso Nino was on the crew of the ship with Columbus. Negroes explored the new world with Balboa and Cortes. Estevanico helped explore the Southwest for the Spanish discoverers. Blacks explored the North and South American continents with the Spanish and French long before the English settlers came to the new world.

Because he came to the new land, the Negro can be called an immigrant. But he was not like the European immigrants. Most Negroes were brought to the new world as slaves. They did not choose to come. They were captured and sold in Africa. About half of them died on the journey to America. Several million people were brought in chains to the new world. They had no hopes for the future in the new land. Nevertheless, they helped build the new land and contributed to the new American culture.

The first shipload of Negroes landed at Jamestown in 1619. Because the ships took so long to cross the ocean, many of these people were dirty, sick, and poorly-fed when they reached America. Many died on the trip. These first blacks were indentured servants. Other free blacks came from the West Indies. Many Europeans, as well as Africans, were also indentured servants. Some of them had been lawbreakers in their native lands.

After the first Negroes arrived, new laws made Negroes slaves, persons who could be bought and sold by others. This meant they could not be freed as could indentured servants. For the next 150 years more than 200,000 Negroes were brought to America. Finally in 1807, Congress passed a law. It stated that no more Negro slaves could be brought into the United States. Nevertheless, Negroes continued to be smuggled into the country in large numbers from Africa, the West Indies, and Latin America.

The South wanted slaves for labor. Negroes worked as field workers on big plantations and as servants and craftsmen. Most Negroes came from the hot climate of Africa. Many landowners in the South thus believed that Negroes could work better in the warm climate of the South than the white servants. The most common jobs were clearing the land, planting, and harvesting.

Most Negroes came to America as slaves. They were brought in slave ships until a law was passed in 1807 that stopped the slave trade.

Jean Baptiste du Sable established a trading post on the Chicago River. He remained there for many years and is considered the first settler of the city of Chicago.

By the 1800's, the Negro became the main labor supply on the big southern plantations, and 90 percent of the Negroes lived in the South. While the lives of Negroes as slaves were limited, they nevertheless had a great effect on the South. They helped mold much of the language and many of the customs.

How did the free Negroes help America?

Not all Negroes were slaves. Some were free. Most of the free Negroes lived in the North. One of the most famous Negro settlers was Jean Baptiste Pointe du Sable (1745-1818), a French Negro who came from Haiti. He was the first permanent settler in the Chicago area. Pointe du Sable settled near the mouth of the Chicago River. Others who had come to this area were visitors who preached or traded or explored the land. They did not plan to stay and make their home there. In 1779, Pointe du Sable built a house where he stayed many years. He raised cattle and traded with the Indians. He was one of the first people to settle and live on land that is now Chicago.

Crispus Attucks was killed by British soldiers in the Boston Massacre. Many other Negroes fought against Great Britain in the Revolutionary War.

Pointe du Sable had a very successful trading post. The Indians trusted him. He was a man with a good education and fine tastes. Many visitors and travelers were guests in his well-furnished home in the wilderness.

What part did the Negro play during and after the American Revolution?

Americans fought for their freedom from England in 1776. Nearly 5,000 Negroes fought in that war. Some served as seamen in the navy. Others were in the army. Some received their freedom for fighting in the war. A Negro, Crispus Attucks (1723?-1770), was the first American to be killed by English soldiers. The killing of Attucks and other colonists became known as the Boston Massacre. This was one of several events that led to the American Revolution. At the Battle of Bunker Hill, Peter Salem made himself known as an excellent soldier.

After the Revolutionary War, the United States grew westward. Most of the Negroes were still slaves in the South. But some free Negroes moved west. Negro families looked for freedom on the frontier. The West was a good place to prove oneself. It took a strong man to withstand the hardships of frontier living.

Negroes rode trails and drove cattle along with other cowboys to Dodge City and Abilene. Some Negroes joined the great Gold Rush to California in 1849.

Many Negroes were able to find freedom by moving west. Some were hunters, mountain men, and trappers.

What part did the Negro have in the Civil War?

By 1860 there were four and a half million Negroes in America. Only a half million were free. The others were still slaves. The life of a slave was not easy. Most worked long, hard hours with little hope for the future. Free Negroes joined other citizens in the Abolition Movement which was an attempt to end slavery. Many people believed that slavery was wrong. Some Abolitionists started the Underground Railroad. This was a planned escape route for slaves. People would make hiding places or "stations" for them. Here runaway slaves were given food and rest. Then they would be taken to the next "station." They would go from station to station until they reached safety. The Underground Railroad ran from the South to Canada. Thousands of Negroes escaped from slavery in this way. Most settled in the northern states. Others went all the way to Canada.

Many people, both Negro and white, helped slaves escape from the South on the Underground Railroad.

One of the outstanding Negroes in the Abolition Movement was Frederick Douglass (1817?-1895). He was born into slavery, but educated himself. When he was twenty years old, Douglass escaped to the North. He spoke before many groups of people in churches and meeting halls and became well known all over the North. In his speeches, Douglass tried to make others understand that slavery was wrong because it was not in keeping with our democratic principles of equality.

The man who had been Douglass' former owner threatened to take him back down South as a slave. Douglass fled to England where he stayed for two years. Some friends bought his freedom so that he could return to the United States without fear of capture. Douglass started a newspaper and continued his fight against the evils of slavery.

When the Civil War began, Douglass visited President Lincoln, and they became friends. He asked President Lincoln to allow Negro soldiers to help fight. More than 150,000 Negroes fought in the Civil War. It was during the Civil War that Lincoln signed the Emancipation Proclamation which gave freedom to the Negroes.

Frederick Douglass meets some of his friends and well-wishers in his office in Washington, D.C.

What changes were made after the Civil War?

After the Civil War, Negroes were free. But many of them stayed in the South and continued doing the same work they had done before the war. Most of them had little education. They were in debt to the man who owned the farmland. They found it hard to get any other kind of job. They found it hard to keep their rights of citizenship in the South.

Negro people began looking for a better way of life. During World Wars I and II, new jobs opened in northern cities. Thousands of Negroes moved from the South to these new jobs. Here in the big cities Negroes met new problems. Housing was poor and crowded. There was only one section of the city where they were allowed to live. Working in factories was very different from working on farms. The climate was cold. Then, too, Negroes were not readily accepted by their new northern neighbors. But there was greater opportunity for education and better jobs. In the North the people could also vote in the elections. Civil rights movements helped bring about laws to insure the rights of Negroes . These laws give the Negro the rights that all Americans should have.

Who are some of the outstanding Negroes in America?

An important citizen in early America was Benjamin Banneker (1731-1806). He was a free Negro who taught himself mathematics and astronomy. Banneker wrote an <u>almanac</u>, a yearbook or calendar giving the days of the week and months and facts about the moon and sun. It was published each year for eleven years. Because of his talents, Banneker was asked by President George Washington to help plan the capital city of Washington, D.C.

Booker T. Washington was a famous Negro educator. He established Tuskegee Institute in Alabama. A famous Negro scientist, George Washington Carver, discovered hundreds of uses for peanuts and sweet potatoes.

In the field of education, Mary McLeod Bethune (1875-1955) founded the Bethune-Cookman College in Daytona Beach, Florida, and became an advisor to both President Roosevelt and President Truman. W. E. B. DuBois was the first Negro to get a Doctor of Philosophy degree from Harvard University. He wrote of the problems of the Negro and worked for laws that would give the Negro the same rights as other citizens.

Negroes are well known through their work in the arts. Marion Anderson (1902-) became one of the great concert and opera singers of the world. Henry O. Tanner (1859-1937) won many awards for his religious paintings. Gwendolyn Brooks (1917-) was awarded the Pulitzer Prize for her poetry.

Leontyne Price sang the leading role in "Cleopatra" for the opening of the Lincoln Center of the Performing Arts in New York.

Leontyne Price, a famous opera singer, opened the new Metropolitan Opera House in New York in 1966. She sang the lead role in "Cleopatra," an opera written just for her.

Dr. Ralph Bunche was an American statesman. He worked for many years with the United Nations. He has received worldwide recognition for his great work in settling the Arab Israeli fighting.

In 1966 Robert Weaver became the first Negro to be chosen for the cabinet of the President of the United States. He became the first Secretary of Urban Affairs. Edward W. Brooke was elected U.S. Senator from Massachusetts in 1966. This was the first time in one hundred years that a Negro was elected to this high office.

Dr. Ralph Bunche received the Nobel Peace Prize in 1950 for his role in settling the Arab-Israeli War.

Young blacks are serving their country with honor in the armed forces. One among many who gave his life in Viet Nam for his country was Private Milton L. Olive III (1948-1966). Olive Park in Chicago is dedicated to him and to other servicemen who gave their lives in war.

Two well-known organizations are the National Association for the Advancement of Colored People (NAACP) and the Urban League. Many outstanding black leaders have worked with these organizations to further the rights of black people. Among these leaders are Roy Wilkins and the late Whitney M. Young. Thurgood Marshall has had a distinguished law career. In 1967 he became an associate justice of the Supreme Court.

What problems do blacks have today?

Minority means the smaller part or number. It is the opposite of the majority, or larger part or number. Immigrant groups have been considered minority groups. But after people have been in America for a long time, they often lose their old minority identity. Foreign names are sometimes changed, and the foreign languages are often not spoken by younger generations. In the case of the Afro-American, it has been impossible for him to lose his minority label. After centuries of living in America, Afro-Americans are still regarded by many people as our oldest and largest minority group. The young generation of today pays no attention to this minority status and refuses to let it stand in the way of progress. They take great pride in their race and their cultural background. The terms "Negro" and "colored" are used less than in past years. Instead, Afro-Americans now are proud to call themselves "blacks." The motto, "Black is Beautiful," has helped give them pride in their identity. The study of African history also helps provide a greater feeling of having firm roots in a very old and a very honorable culture, that of their native land.

Like the waves of immigrants coming from Europe, waves of Afro-Americans moved from the South to the North in search of better jobs and education. As did the Irish, Germans, Poles, and Italians, they settled in segregated communities. Harlem in New York City was like "Little Italy" at the turn of the century. But the Afro-Americans have met even stronger prejudice than did the immigrants of the last century. The black man has had to face the possibility that he and his children and grandchildren may always live in the same segregated environment.

These children live in the Harlem area of New York City. They have very little place to play.

Many leaders have worked very hard in the movement to gain a better life for all blacks. New laws have been passed through the efforts of blacks and whites, men and women, to end discrimination in education, housing, and public services. Many blacks have found great success and recognition because of their talents. For millions of others, the escape to better housing, education, and jobs is hard to make. These problems can be helped by working to end poverty, crowding, crime, and unemployment.

Roy Wilkins believes in friendship and understanding between blacks and whites. He works hard for this ideal.

With the help of Presidents Eisenhower, Kennedy, and Johnson, the Congress of the United States has passed <u>civil rights</u> laws. Civil rights are those rights of personal liberty guaranteed to American citizens by the Constitution or by acts of Congress. These recent laws have provided for fairness to all in business, education, and housing. There is still a long way to go to find the ways to improve the lives of thousands of blacks. The words of the late President, John F. Kennedy, spell out the hopes for all black Americans.

"This is one country. It has become one country because all of us and all the people who came here had an equal chance to develop their talents. We cannot say to ten percent of the population that they can't have that right; that their children can't have the chance to develop whatever talents they have; that the only way that they are going to get their rights is to go into the streets and demonstrate. I think we owe them and we owe ourselves a better country than that."

One black who will always be remembered by millions of people was Martin Luther King, Jr. He spent his whole life trying to improve the living conditions of blacks. King traveled all over America. He also visited India, West Africa, Latin America, and many places in Europe. On these trips he talked to government leaders about the importance of civil rights and how to be sure all people really had equal rights.

Martin Luther King was born in Atlanta, Georgia in 1929. His father and grandfather were Baptist ministers and he became one also. A firm believer in the benefits of education, he earned a doctor of philosophy degree from Boston University. King went on to organize and become president of the Southern Christian Leadership Conference, a group which works hard for equal rights for all people. As the leader of this group, Dr. King led long marches and peaceful demonstrations in the South. He showed all people the injustices in society. Dr. King always insisted that violence was not needed in the fight for equal rights. In 1964 he won the Nobel Peace Prize for leadership in the peaceful struggle for racial equality in America.

Dr. and Mrs. Martin Luther King, Jr. smile with pleasure as he accepts the Nobel Peace Prize for his work in civil rights.

This hard-working black, a true lover of mankind, was killed by an assassin in 1968, but his memory and inspiration continue to live. Americans remember the dream of Dr. King who said:

"Even though we face the difficulties of today and tomorrow, I still have a dream. It is a dream chiefly rooted in the American dream. I have a dream that one day this nation will rise up and live out the true meaning of its creed: 'We hold these truths to be self-evident, that all men are created equal.'

"I have a dream that one day, on the red hills of Georgia, the sons of former slaves and the sons of former slave owners will be able to sit down together at the table of brotherhood. . ."

WHAT WOULD YOU DO?

Suppose you were a leader such as Dr. Martin Luther King in a black, inner-city community. You want to help bring better housing, more jobs, better medical and educational services, and an end to crime in the community.

1. How might you begin to work with the people in your community?
2. How could you get the help of young people, city officials, state officials, and business leaders?
3. What will be some of the problems you will meet?
4. What would you say to the community people to give them hope and a feeling of confidence and pride?
5. What black leaders in sports, politics, business, education, and science might you call on for advice and support? How could they help you?

WHAT DO YOU THINK?

1. In what ways were the problems of the blacks of long ago similar to the problems of the European immigrants? In what ways were they different?
2. Why do many young blacks want to leave rural parts of the south to live in northern cities? Do you think they find a better life in big cities?
3. How can they prepare themselves for a city job?
4. Why is Martin Luther King greatly honored?

5. How were the lives of the early blacks like those of the European indentured servants in early America? How were their lives different?
6. Why do you think it is important to learn African History?
7. Why do you think most blacks wish to have strong community organizations to help them live better?
8. How can such organizations help improve schools, health services, and services such as police and transportation?

9. What is meant by the "Civil Rights Movement"? Do civil rights marches help the blacks? Why?
10. How have Supreme Court decisions helped blacks in their fight for equal rights?
11. What are housing problems in urban communities where many blacks live?

Immigrants from Other Cultural Groups

What did the Chinese contribute to America?

The discovery of gold in California brought the first wave of Chinese immigrants to the United States in 1848. At first only a few Chinese merchants came to sell their tea and other goods to the miners and settlers. Then they wrote home telling about the gold in California. By 1851 there were 25,000 Chinese on the west coast of America. Ten years later, there were 35,000. Many Chinese immigrants did not leave their homeland to escape, but rather to earn money and return home to preserve their way of life.

In mining camps, the Chinese stayed by themselves. Their appearance and their ways were different. The American miners did not accept them as friends. Some Chinese looked for gold and a few became rich with their gold strikes. But most Chinese found that working in a service job was a surer way of earning money. The Chinese took such jobs as housekeepers, gardeners, and laundrymen. Some worked in labor jobs on railroads and in mines.

This train trestle in the Sierra Nevada Mountains in California was completed by Chinese laborers in 1877.

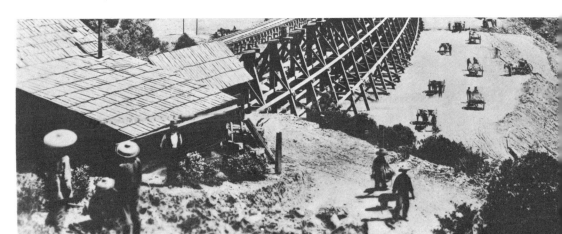

The railroads and other employers paid the Chinese less than other workers. The Chinese would work for less pay because it was still much more than they had earned in China. There were many jobs as long as the gold rush in California lasted. When the gold rush ended, it was difficult to find a job.

Immigrants from China wore clothing and hair styles that were quite different from other immigrants.

Because the customs of the Chinese were different, they were not always understood by other people. Their clothes were different. Their language was different. The queue, or long pigtail, they wore was different.

In 1882 the Chinese Exclusion Act was passed. This law stopped the Chinese from coming to America for ten years. People who were born in China were not allowed to become citizens of the United States. It was not until 1943 that the exclusion act was changed. The Chinese were then given a quota of 105 immigrants each year. This law marked the first time that the American government had stopped the people of one country from coming here. Many Chinese left America during this time.

A large number of those who remained in this country left the West Coast. They developed neighborhoods of their own in cities such as Chicago, Detroit, and New York. These neighborhoods are called Chinatown. Some of the old Chinese traditions still remain there, but now Chinatown is changing. Chinese laundries are disappearing. The stores do not have as many Chinese goods to sell.

The traditional dragon leads the parade through Chinatown as part of the Chinese New Year celebration.

Chinese restaurants seem to do the most business. Some of the interesting dishes they serve include pickled Chinese cabbage, shark fin soup, dumplings, and almond cookies.

Older Chinese people usually remain in Chinatown. Their children move away and find jobs in business, medicine, and law. But the Chinese have not lost all their traditions. Some still learn to read and speak Chinese in special classes. Many Chinese return to Chinatown for celebrations such as the Chinese New Year.

When the Communists came to power on China's mainland in 1949, the ties with America were broken. Only the Chinese Nationalists on Formosa continued to be friendly. However, through the Refugee Relief Act of 1953, Chinese and other Far Eastern refugees were admitted to the United States. In 1970 eight thousand new Chinese immigrants came here.

The pipe Ah Louis is shown smoking is very unusual in America. It probably came from China long ago.

Who are some of the well-known Chinese-Americans?

Ah Louis was a Chinese businessman. When he first came to the United States he helped get jobs for the Chinese people who had wanted to come to America. Many of these Chinese were among those who built our great railroads. Later, Ah Louis built his own store in California. Today that store has been named an historical landmark, honoring Ah Louis and all Chinese-Americans.

Lyman Jee was born at a time when the Chinese people could not buy land. Today Mr. Jee is an architect and land developer. He owns many buildings and landsites. Another successful businessman is Sinclair Louie. His father had a small curio shop, or store which sells unsual things, in San Francisco's Chinatown. Mr. Louie worked hard to make his father's business grow. Today he is the owner of many large stores. He also owns the famous Chinatown Wax Museum.

Dr. Thomas Hum is on the staff of the Chinese Hospital in San Francisco. He has worked tirelessly to obtain medical care for poor Chinese. Two other doctors, T. D. Lee, of Columbia University, and C. N. Yang, of the State University of New York, shared the 1957 Nobel Prize for physics. Dr. C. S. Wu, of Columbia University, is a woman scientist. She is known all through the medical world as a foremost experimental physicist.

116

How have the Japanese contributed to American life?

In about 1900, a large number of Japanese immigrants came to the United States. Before 1886, fewer than eighty Japanese had come here in any one year. But in 1907, over 30,000 Japanese came to the United States. They came because Japan did not have enough food or jobs for them. First the Japanese went to work on the Hawaiian sugar plantations. Then others went to California. Many found jobs as household help, miners, and lumberers.

The Japanese wanted to follow American ways and become good Americans. They learned these ways very quickly and helped build our growing nation. In 1941 the United States and Japan went to war. In America those with Japanese backgrounds were feared and ordered to leave their homes and businesses. They were sent to ten relocation centers in various western and plains states. They had to stay there during the war and were looked after by the United States Army. This is a sad part of our past. We did not trust these people because some were born in another country. Yet more than 12,000 <u>nisei</u> served with honor in the United States Army. These nisei formed the 422nd Regimental Combat Team. Nisei are people born in America of Japanese parents.

Many Japanese-Americans helped defend America during World War II.

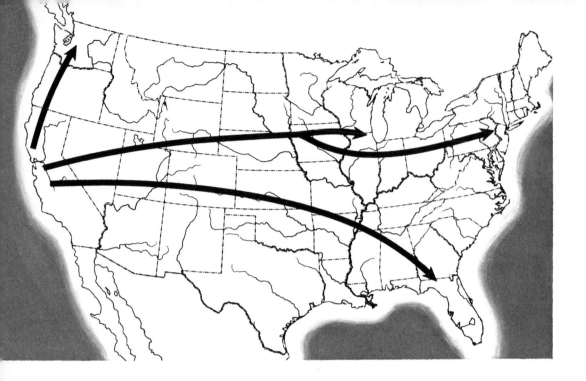

The period following World War II was a time of great readjustment for Japanese-Americans. Many settled in other areas of the United States, rather than return to their former homes. Most of the people had lost all of their money and property. But through hard work, they rebuilt their lives. Other Americans finally recognized the great injustice done to the Japanese-Americans during World War II. The Congress of the United States passed a law which directed the Attorney General of the United States to pay the Japanese-Americans for the losses they suffered because of the relocation. Most of the people, however, had lost more than the government repaid.

One organization which has done much work to help the Japanese-American is the Japanese American Citizens League. It has helped attain civil rights for these loyal citizens. Old laws which prevented citizenship, voting, and owning property no longer exist. Much good has been accomplished since the days of World War II.

Time has overcome the hard feelings other Americans held toward the Japanese-American people. It is hoped that never again will there be a period in our history when the loyalty of a whole group of people will be questioned.

Most of America's larger cities have many very good Japanese restaurants. Some of them are like restaurants in Japan, where the customers take off their shoes and sit on the floor. Would you like to try some of the food shown below?

1. Fish paste	7. Tofu (bean curd)	13. Udo (vegetable)
2. Toro	8. Boiled fish paste	14. Whitefish
3. Chicken	9. Shrimp	15. Chinese cabbage
4. Green peas	10. Oyster	16. Clam
5. Shitake (mushrooms)	11. Fuki (vegetable)	17. Radish
6. Squid	12. Sea eel	18. Ginko nut

Who are some well-known Japanese-Americans?

A well-known architect is Minour Yamasaki, who was born in the United States. He has received many awards and honors for his outstanding architectural designs. Among his many works are the Reynolds Metals Company building in Detroit, the Oberlin College Music Conservatory, the St. Louis Airport, and also the Northwestern National Life Insurance Company building.

Isamu Noguchi is a famous Japanese-American sculptor. Dr. S. I. Hayakawa, teacher and writer, became president of San Francisco State College in 1969. Senator Daniel K. Inouye and Congressman Masayuki Matsunaga are two of the many Japanese-Americans in politics. They are from Hawaii, where Japanese-Americans make up the largest group in the population. Many other Japanese-Americans serve as state senators and as leaders at the many local levels of government.

This building in Minneapolis was designed by Minour Yamasaki. He feels that "We must achieve serenity in our buildings to offset the chaos of our times. . ."

Hideyo Noguchi (1876-1928) was born in Japan. After graduation from Tokyo Medical School, he came to Philadelphia. There he did research work on snake venom.

In 1904 Noguchi moved to New York to work in the Rockefeller Institute for Medical Research. He investigated various diseases and their causes and treatment. Polio and yellow fever were among the illnesses on which he worked.

In 1928 Dr. Noguchi learned that scientists were working in Africa to discover more about yellow fever. He joined them in their search, became ill from that disease, and died in 1928.

WHAT WOULD YOU DO?

Twice in his life, Dr. Noguchi traveled many thousands of miles to help his fellowman. Travel in those days was extremely slow and difficult, if not dangerous. Imagine that you are Dr. Noguchi.

1. What would be your reason for moving to America?
2. Do you think American doctors in those days welcomed doctors from other countries? Why or why not?
3. Yellow fever was common in Africa and no cure was known. Why would you want to go there?

How have people from the Middle East contributed to America?

The Middle East is an area of land located at the meeting point of three continents. Those continents are Europe, Africa, and Asia. The countries included make up an area almost as large as the United States.

Most parts of the Middle East are very poor. Farming methods are the same as they were many years ago. The people do not have enough to eat because most of the land is too dry to grow crops. In some places there are no schools. The children need a better education in order to have a good life.

The number of immigrants to America from these countries is smaller than from most other places. People who do come here from the Middle East have many of the same reasons as have other immigrants. They hope to have a better life here in America than in their homeland.

Organizations have been formed by immigrants from various Middle East countries. They work for better education and jobs for their people, both in America and in their native countries.

There is a bill, or a plan for a new law, that many groups have worked very hard to have passed by Congress. It is an act to start Ethnic Heritage Studies Centers. This bill would provide $30 million for the study of the languages and the cultures of people of different kinds of nationalities.

One of the people who has been active in this work is Sargon D. David. He, as well as many others, feels it is a good thing to learn about and be proud of one's heritage. Mr. David was born in Iraq in 1930. He came to the United States in 1955 as a college student. He is now an American citizen.

Sargon David is a writer and speaker on problems of the Middle East.

One way that Mr. David helps others is by teaching Americanization to those who need or want to learn more about our country. He has worked with the Assyrian American Federation and the Iraqui Students Society in the United States. He is active in government and works for the election of responsible officials.

In 1964 Mr. David returned to northern Iraq as an observer of the war there. When it was time for him to return to America, the government there did not want him to leave. He finally escaped by going through the mountains to the north.

WHAT WOULD YOU DO?

Imagine yourself wanting to escape from your old country. Some people do not want you to go. You decide that you must at least try to get back to your new country.

1. What kind of plan could you make to leave safely?
2. Would you tell anyone your plan?
3. Would you be willing to leave behind your friends and relatives for what you believe is a better place in which to live?
4. Do you think anything could ever happen to make you want to leave your country in this way?

What have Jewish people contributed to America?

The Jews are a religious group like the Catholics and the Protestants. They are also an immigrant group, as are the Irish, Germans, and others. The Jews came to America from many countries. They brought their religious customs with them, as did many other people. These immigrants had a strong bond among themselves even though they came from many different places. They shared the heritage of their religious traditions.

Since their early history, the Jews had often suffered discrimination. The new land offered hope for a better life. The first Jewish settlers came to New Amsterdam in 1654. At the start of the American Revolution, only 2,000 Jews lived in America. They were good citizens. They educated their children and built synagogues, which are the Jewish houses of worship. Haym Solomon, who was a Polish Jew, spent almost his entire fortune during the Revolutionary War. He purchased guns and equipment and paid the salaries of Congressmen.

This family is celebrating the Passover meal. Jewish families celebrate this religious custom as a reminder of their freedom from the Egyptians.

In the 1800's many Jewish immigrants began to come to America. By 1880 there were 300,000 Jews in the United States. The Jews came to escape religious persecution. Most families were too poor to send everyone to America at one time. Usually the father or oldest son would go first, save his money, then send for the family. Sometimes it took many years to reunite a family. "Sleep My Child" is a <u>lullaby,</u> or song, which was written by Sholom Aleichem. In this song a mother sings to her child as they wait for word from the father in America:

Sleep, my child, my sweet, my pretty one,
    Sleep, my darling, sleep.
Sleep, my life, my sweet, my pretty one,
    Sleep, my darling son.

Daddy's gone to America,
    Daddy's gone far away.
He has left us here a-waiting
    Sleep, my darling babe.

Daddy will send us twenty dollars,
    And his picture too.
If he's living, sure he'll fetch us,
    We'll start life anew.

The help given to one's family and friends was like links in a never-ending chain. One person would help another get to America. He, in turn, would help someone new. Fathers, mothers, aunts, uncles, cousins, and even old friends often joined the chain. The old-world bonds of fear, poverty, and religious tradition bound the Jews closely together even in the new world.

The Jewish immigrants settled mostly in large cities. Here they could get jobs quickly. They often moved into neighborhoods that had once been occupied by earlier immigrant groups. The Lower East Side in New York City was once the largest Jewish community. Many prominent Jewish actors and entertainers tell of their early childhood here. Other groups lived in neighborhoods in Chicago, Philadelphia, and Boston. These were crowded areas where people faced poverty and poor working conditions. Yet there was a feeling of great hope among Jewish immigrants.

Furthering education and carrying on their religious and cultural traditions were among the goals of the Jewish immigrants.

Courtesy Chicago Historical Society

Hundreds of small synagogues were built. Religious schools were opened where children learned Hebrew. Public education was also valued by Jewish people. These immigrants joined together to help each other. They started groups to help the poor and aged. They set up homes for orphans and organized hospitals and research centers. Community centers were opened for the recreation of young and old.

A great many Jewish people worked in the garment industry in New York in 1900.

Many German Jews had been tradespeople in their homeland, with their own shops or stores. When they came to America, they often had to start all over. Instead of going to the cities, many of these people became peddlers in the rural areas. They traveled with packs on their backs and sold many goods. Farm people were glad to see the peddlers because stores were too far away to visit often. Soon the peddlers

Peddlers were common long ago.

were able to buy horses and wagons, and their businesses grew. The great fortunes of such people as the Guggenheims and the Rosenwalds were started in this way.

There are nearly six million Jews in the United States today. The waves of immigration in the 1800's and early 1900's brought large numbers of these immigrants to America. World War I stopped the immigration movement. Immigration increased again during World War II. At that time, thousands of Jewish refugees came to the United States.

These refugees came mainly from western Europe. Even though their backgrounds and customs were different, they all came to America for the same reason. They wanted a safer and better place in which to live and raise their families. At the present time, there are still Jewish refugees attempting to leave Russia and other Communist countries. Looking for religious and political freedom, some of these present refugees wish to go to America. Many others would like to go to Israel.

Who have been some outstanding Jewish-Americans?

The talents of many Jewish men and women have helped make the United States a better country. History is filled with the names of Jewish leaders whose work has enriched the nation.

Four men mentioned earlier in our story were Jewish. Their names were Joseph Pulitzer, Casimir Funk, Albert Einstein, and Edward Teller. These people from different nations shared the common heritage of their Jewish culture.

Emma Lazarus was a famous poet. Her best-known poem is found on the Statue of Liberty. You may read the poem on page 176. Lillian Wald was one of the first public health nurses. She worked for many years to better the living conditions and health of immigrants in New York.

Three Jewish men who became Justices of the Supreme Court were Louis D. Brandeis, Benjamin Cardozo, and Felix Frankfurter.

Dr. Jonas Salk developed the Salk vaccine to prevent polio. He saved countless numbers of people from suffering and death.

The entertainment world owes much to the Jewish people. Composers George Gershwin and Oscar Hammerstein II wrote many famous songs. Arthur Miller has written great plays. One of the best-loved comedians in the world is Mr. Jack Benny.

Lillian Wald founded the Henry Street settlement for social services in New York. She also worked with the Red Cross.

Oscar Hammerstein (ca. 1847-1919). The abbreviation "ca." is for "circa," which means "about." It comes from the Latin word circum. In this story, it means Mr. Hammerstein's exact year of birth is unknown.

Oscar Hammerstein was the grandfather of the composer mentioned earlier. He was born in Germany and came to the United States in 1863. He soon made a fortune in the tobacco business.

Mr. Hammerstein became interested in the theater. He built several theaters and opera houses in New York City, Philadelphia, and London. His Manhattan Opera House in New York was a rival of the Metropolitan Opera House for many years. Hammerstein became well-known as an inventor, composer, theater manager, and supporter of the opera.

WHAT WOULD YOU DO?

Hammerstein, a German Jew, was about sixteen when he came to America. He later became a world traveler to accomplish his successes. He was a well-known lover of the opera.

1. Do you think Oscar learned his love for and knowledge of the opera in Germany or America?
2. How do you think Oscar felt when his opera house failed? Would it bother him only in the "pocket book"?
3. Oscar Hammerstein died shortly before his grandson became famous. Do you think he had helped his namesake in his career? In what way?

WHAT DO YOU THINK?

1. Name a country in the Far East from which immigrants come to America.
2. Why did Oriental immigrants in the 1900's have greater problems than the European immigrants?
3. Why do many Jewish children in the United States still attend Hebrew class after school?

4. Why was the war with Japan during World War II especially hard for many Japanese-Americans? How did the American government try to make up to the Japanese-Americans for their suffering and losses during the war?
5. Why do you think the Chinatown areas developed in many big cities? Why are these big city Chinatown areas changing now?

6. Why did many early Chinese immigrants work as cooks and laundry men instead of mining for gold so they could become rich quickly?
7. Why were the Jewish people anxious to escape from Germany when the Nazis were in power?
8. Why are exchanges of students, scientists, and artists between countries important for people of those countries?

The Mexican Americans Helped Build The United States

Who are the Mexican Americans?

There are at least six million Mexican American people living in the southwestern United States. Most of them live in Texas, New Mexico, Colorado, Arizona, and California. There are also Mexican Americans in cities in other states. Chicago, Detroit, Gary, and Kansas City have large numbers of Mexican Americans who either moved there from the Southwest or immigrated from Mexico.

Mexican Americans are descendants of the Spanish, Indian, and Mexican people. During the many years when these people settled the Southwest, these groups became mixed. A few Mexican Americans can trace their forefathers directly to the early Spanish settlers. They settled in the Southwest as long as 400 years ago.

Some Mexican Americans call themselves Hispano Americans to point out their Spanish heritage. Most of these people live in northern New Mexico, Colorado, and California. Many times Mexican Americans are called Spanish-speaking people or Latin Americans. Some Mexican Americans like to be called <u>chicanos</u>.

This pinata is part of our Mexican heritage. Pinatas are filled with candy and hung from the ceiling, to be broken by children as part of Christmas festivities.

The Mexican American culture is different in some ways from that of other Americans. Many customs of these people came from the Spanish and Indian cultures. Most Mexican Americans speak two languages, Spanish and English. They have very close family relationships. Sometimes the needs of the whole family will come before those of one person in the family. Some Mexican Americans enjoy different foods, music, and folktales than do many other Americans.

The Mexican American way of life was well-established when settlers from other areas of the country arrived in the Southwest about 150 years ago. The Mexican Americans have kept many of their old customs and habits, but they have also adopted many new ways. In the same way, Mexican American traditions and cultural habits have become part of the American way of life. Spanish and Indian influences can be found in buildings, music, words, laws, and food. Many of their ways of farming, mining, and cattle and sheep raising have become part of our heritage.

Spanish, the language of many Mexican Americans, has enriched the language of the people of the United States. Cities from St. Augustine, Florida, to San Francisco, California, have Spanish names. The names of the states of California, Florida, Colorado, Montana, and Nevada are Spanish. New Mexico, Arizona, and Texas have names that come from Indian words that were changed to make them sound Spanish.

ENGLISH	SPANISH	ENGLISH	SPANISH
airplane	aeroplano	mesquite	mezquite
avocado	aguacate	tamale	tamal
chocolate	chocolate	tomato	tomate
coyote	coyote	tourist	turista
chicle	chicle	train	tren
chili	chile	transportation	transporte
immigrant	immigrante	traveler	viajero

Los Primeros (Los Pree-'meh-ros), or the first settlers, made charts and maps of the land in the Southwest. Hundreds of streams, rivers, mountain ranges, lakes, and forests have Spanish names. The word canyon is Spanish, as is mesa, a flat-topped mountain. An arroyo is a large gully which is dry most of the time. The Sierra Nevada mountains of California, and the rivers, Rio Grande, Colorado, and Gila all have Spanish names. The Gulf of Mexico washes the southern shores of the United States.

The Pacific Ocean was named by Vasco Nunez de Balboa of Spain. He named it El Mar Pacifico (El Mahr Pah-'see-fee-co), which means "the peaceful sea." The names of ocean bays, ports, and islands such as Matagordo Bay, Port Lavaca, and Padre Island in Texas are Spanish-named.

Some words that are in common use in the United States today are combinations of Spanish and Indian words. On the chart above are words in Spanish and English. See how much alike they are. Can you name others?

Why did the forefathers of the Mexican Americans settle in the American Southwest?

In 1520 Hernando Cortez conquered the Aztec Indians in Mexico. Soon reports came back to Mexico City that there was much gold in the lands to the north. Tales of the Seven Cities of Gold excited the Spaniards. Francisco Vasquez de Coronado was sometimes called the "Knight of Pueblos and Plains." He led a large group of explorers who went to find the legendary cities. He did not find the cities, but his group explored much of northern Mexico and the southwestern United States. One of Coronado's captains discovered the Grand Canyon in Arizona.

More than forty years later, the Spaniards sent Don Juan de Onate to lead a group of soldiers, Indians, and missionaries, or priests. He explored the regions of the upper Rio Grande (great river). He called the territory Nuevo Mexico and became the first governor of this area. Onate started the pueblo, or town, of San Juan de los Caballeros in 1598.

In about 1610 another governor made La Villa Real de Santa Fe the capital of Nuevo Mexico. It is the oldest state capital in the United States. Santa Fe is the second oldest city founded by Europeans in the United States. The oldest city is St. Augustine, Florida. St. Augustine was founded as a fortress by the Spaniards in 1565.

Juan Rodrigues Cabrillo gave Spain her claim to California. He sailed northward in the Pacific Ocean to look for the "island" of California. He landed at Point Loma in the bay of San Diego. He later discovered the bay of Santa Monica near the present city of Los Angeles.

Spaniards also explored and settled Texas. Alvan Nunez Cabeza de Vaca was an early explorer of Texas. He and other Spaniards were shipwrecked on the Texas coast. Only four men survived. One of them was Cabeza de Vaca. They made friends with the Indians and lived with them. These men traveled across much of Texas. When they finally got back to Mexico City, they told the stories they had heard about the Seven Cities of Cibola.

Other countries were interested in becoming landowners in the New World. The English, French, and Russians made explorations near the Spanish lands. When the Spanish kings heard of this, they sent soldiers and settlers to colonize and guard the land. Missionaries went with them to convert the Indians, or make them Christians. The Spanish felt that if the Indians became Christians, they would help protect the Spanish lands.

The earliest settlements were started in northern New Mexico. Here the Spaniards found many Indians living in pueblos. Their homes were made of clay. Some were more than one story high. The Spaniards built missions and presidios, or small forts, near these pueblos. Sometimes they built their own pueblos, such as

The sketch below shows a typical presidio of the 19th century. They were used for protection from Indian attacks. Presidios were an important part of new settlements.

Mission Delores was built in 1776. Life in the mission was busy. Priests helped the Indians learn to be farmers and craftsmen.

the village of Santa Fe. The settlement, made up of the presidio, the mission, and the pueblo, became the center for spreading Spanish culture. It was here that the culture of the Spaniards and the Indians began creating the Mexican heritage.

Many people believe that the work of the priests was the most important contribution of the Spaniards in settling frontiers. They paved the way for future settlers. The missionaries taught the Indians the Christian religion. They also showed them how to grow many plants which they had brought from Spain and Mexico. They taught them how to raise sheep, goats, and cattle. The missionaries blazed new trails in the wilderness, made maps of the country, and described the new land in reports and letters.

The missions were the beginnings of later settlements. Over two hundred years ago there were more than one hundred Spanish missions in California, Arizona, New Mexico, and Texas. Many of the settlements built near the missions became large cities: in California there are the cities of San Francisco and Los Angeles; in Texas are San Antonio and El Paso; New Mexico has Santa Fe and Albuquerque; Tucson and Phoenix are cities in Arizona.

One well-known missionary was Father Junipero Serra, who started at least nine missions in California. Another important missionary was Father Eusebio Kino in Arizona. Father Kino was called the "Padre on Horseback." He rode a mustang horse.

The Alamo was a fort built to defend the mission of San Antonio in Texas. In 1836 it was attacked by General Santa Ana of Mexico. Many men died.

How did the Southwest become part of the United States?

Until 1821 Mexico belonged to Spain. But the people were not happy with the Spanish government. They revolted and won their independence. The country became the Republic of Mexico. Soon people in the United States became interested in these Mexican lands. They were especially interested in East Texas because it had good land for farming. Many families moved to Texas. Later, these Americans and some of the Mexicans in Texas did not like the way the Mexican government treated them. They revolted against Mexico. As a result, the fort called the Alamo was attacked by 4,000 men. The battle lasted twelve days and all of the men defending it, about 185, were killed.

After Texas won her independence in 1836, she had arguments with Mexico over the location of the boundary between them. In 1846 Texas joined the United States. When Texas became part of the United States, the boundary arguments grew worse. The United States declared war on Mexico in 1846 and defeated her in 1848.

After the Mexican War, the United States gained the land that later became California, Arizona, Nevada, Utah, New Mexico, and part of Colorado. The people who lived there had been citizens of Mexico. The Treaty of Guadalupe-Hidalgo gave them the choice of moving into Mexico or becoming citizens of the United States. Most chose to stay on the land that had been their home for hundreds of years. They became citizens of the United States.

What did the Spanish and Mexicans contribute to the people of the United States?

The first people in the Southwest, other than Indians, were the European settlers. When settlers from the eastern United States arrived, they found much of the land already occupied and settled. The Hispanos, or Spaniards, and the Mexicans had learned much from the Indians about how to live in the Southwest. They also had brought many ideas with them from Spain. Much of the land in the Southwest was like the land in Spain. It had few trees and little rainfall, except in the mountain ranges that rose from the desert floors.

The Spanish had learned how to irrigate, or water, their big fields. Where rivers and streams flowed into the dry valleys, the people would build small dams and acequias (a-'seh-kee-uhs), or ditches. These carried the water into fields along the banks. The main canal that carried water from the stream to the pueblo was called the acequia madre ('mah-dre), or mother canal. Small ditches led from the main canal to each piece of land. Each field was a square with dirt walls around it to hold the water. As each square was soaked, an opening was made in the side wall and the water flowed into the next small field.

Lack of water was a serious problem for early settlers in the Southwest.

Adobe buildings were common in the Southwest because of the materials available.

Since there were few trees for building homes, churches, and presidios in the Southwest, early settlers used <u>adobe</u>. Adobe is a mixture of clay, soil, and straw. It is mixed with water until it is very soft mud. Then it is poured into a mold to dry into bricks. Adobes were put together with mud. The adobe building was then roofed with beams and covered with branches. Over these were poured layers of dirt. Adobe buildings were warm in the winter, cool in summer.

The Spaniards brought cattle, sheep, and horses with them to the new world. Raising these animals became a very important industry in the Southwest. The cattle often escaped their owners and roamed in the wilds. In what is now southeast Texas, cattle ran wild in the <u>chaparral,</u> or brush country. When the need for beef increased in the eastern United States, the cattle were rounded up. Then they were moved along trails to the railroads in Kansas and Missouri.

The American cowboy learned much of his trade from the Mexican <u>vaquero</u> (va-'ker-oh). The vaquero had been important to Spanish ranching for years. The Texas cowboy took over the vaquero's special way of dressing. The <u>sombrero</u>, a large-brimmed hat, protected him from the sun. Leather <u>chapparreras</u> (chah-pohr-'re-rahs), chaps, protected his legs. His high-heeled <u>botas</u> ('bot-taz), boots, kept his feet from slipping through the stirrups.

La reata (lah re-'ah-tah) was changed to "lasso." The practice of rounding up cattle once a year to brand them was called a rodeo. The Spanish rancho became the ranch, and the owner of the ranch, the ranchero, or rancher.

Almost every group of Spanish settlers brought sheep with it. They came with Juan de Onate to northern New Mexico in 1598. In 1681 colonists near the present city of El Paso, Texas, brought sheep with them. Sheep-raising became important in New Mexico and western Texas. The Mexicans herded the churros ('chur-rohs), scrubby, but very hardy, sheep. Burros and dogs helped them. The sheepherder was called un pastor (oon pahs-'tohr).

One of the reasons the Spanish explored new lands was to search for valuable metals. When they conquered Mexico they found that the Indians had much gold and silver. The Spanish used their knowledge of mining to find and work new mines in Mexico.

Methods used by American miners in the gold and silver strikes, or bonanzas, were learned from Mexican miners. They taught the Americans placer mining. Gravel from stream beds was placed in a batea (bat-'te-ah), or wooden bowl, and washed until only the gold was left. Later, when copper became an important metal, Mexicans worked the great open-pit mines in the Southwest.

These prospectors of the 19th century hoped to find a fortune in gold.

The Spaniards and the Mexicans blazed many valuable trails and roads throughout the Southwest. A main road was called a Camino Real (Cah-'mee-no Re-'ahl), or the Royal Road. There were several important ones. Find two on the map above.

When the Southwest became part of the United States, Mexican Americans became important leaders in the government. In California, they helped write the first state constitution. Many of the delegates to the state constitutional convention were Mexican Americans. Among them were Jose Carrillo, Manual Dominguez, Pablo de la Guerra, and General Mariano Vallejo.

In 1836 fifty-nine delegates met to write a declaration of independence and a constitution for the Texas republic. Three of the delegates were of Mexican descent. Two were Jose Ruiz and Jose Navarro. When Texas became a state, in 1845, Navarro was elected to the state senate. A third delegate, Lorenzo de Zavela, later became the first vice-president of Texas.

141

Why did so many Mexican people come to America after 1900?

After the Mexican War ended, thousands of <u>Anglo</u> Americans flocked to California and to Texas. Mexican Americans think of Anglos as any American who is not Mexican, and is of the white race. Soon the Mexican Americans became a minority group in the Southwest, except in New Mexico.

Many of them were large landowners. But often they did not have the documents to prove their ownership and many lost their land. Some Mexicans stayed on as cowboys and sheepherders on ranches. Some went to work for the railroads. Others worked in mines and factories. In Texas many became seasonal workers in the cotton fields. Until 1900 there were fewer than 100,000 Mexican Americans living in the Southwest.

Several events in Mexico and in the United States caused over one million Mexicans to immigrate to the United States. In 1902 the United States Congress passed a law to help farmers build large dams and irrigation systems in the Southwest. This made it possible for millions of acres of land to be used for farming. The valleys in Arizona, California, and Texas produced many fruits and vegetables. These were shipped East in refrigerated railroad cars. In Colorado and nearby states, sugar beets were grown.

Farmers and fruit growers needed all the workers they could hire to raise and harvest these products. There was not enough labor in the United States to do the work. Many people in Mexico heard about these jobs. It was very easy to come to the United States. Railroads connected Mexico with the United States and the tickets were not expensive. There were no quota laws to keep the Mexicans from immigrating to America.

Other events caused many more Mexicans to come to the United States. In 1911, revolutions broke out in Mexico. For ten years there was much fighting among different men who wanted to become the president of Mexico. Some people feared for their lives and left Mexico for political reasons. Others became unhappy with the constant fighting and great poverty. They came here to join their friends and relatives. By 1920, there were at least one and one-half million Mexican Americans living in the United States.

What have been some of the problems faced by Mexican Americans?

Following the Mexican War, there was distrust between Mexican Americans and Anglos. Anglos did not understand the Mexican customs or language. They often felt that Mexican Americans should give up the Spanish language and speak only English.

Mexican Americans experienced much prejudice. They often had to attend separate schools or they were placed in segregated classes. In some places, they could not eat in the same restaurants as Anglos. Often they were not able to buy homes in Anglo neighborhoods, because they did not have enough money, or because they were not wanted there. Some businesses would not hire Mexican Americans. Since many Mexican Americans had little education, they received the lowest-paying jobs.

These men fought for good government. The flag says "Democracy or Death" and "Down with Tyranny."

What is life like in the city for Mexican Americans today?

For years many Mexican Americans have lived in separate neighborhoods. These neighborhoods in the cities are called bar-rios ('bahr-ree-ohs). When the Mexican American neighborhood was located in a rural area, the settlement was called a colonia (co-'lo-nee-ah). Many barrios have large tenement houses called presidios. The presidio may be built in a square with a patio or courtyard in the center. The apartments in the presidios often have only two or three rooms. There may not be running water or a bathroom in the apartment. Often among the tenement houses there are brightly painted cottages with small flower gardens. Individual families live in these.

Some people have lived in the barrios many years. They like to live near other people who have the same customs, music, and food, and are of the same religion. Almost everyone here speaks Spanish. Signs on the small stores and shops are often in Spanish. As one walks through the barrio, Mexican music can be heard on the radios and record players. In border cities, the television may be tuned to a Mexican station.

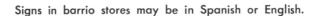

Signs in barrio stores may be in Spanish or English.

Menus in Mexican American restaurants have many delicious foods listed.

ANTOJITOS MEXICANOS (Fiesta Plates)

TACOS—Crisp, folded and stuffed with beef or chicken, lettuce and tomatoes.

ENCHILADAS—Soft, rolled, and stuffed with beef, chicken, or cheese. Topped with melted Mexican cheese and Mexican dark sauce.

TAMALES—Steamed and served in corn husks, stuffed with beef and sauce. Spanish rice and "frijoles" served with each.

Almost every block has a <u>tienda</u> (tee-'en-dah), or small corner grocery store. Special Mexican foods and spices can be bought here. People in the barrio find it pleasant to shop at the tienda because the owner knows each customer. Newspapers printed in Spanish can be bought in the barrio, and movie theaters show Mexican films. Other businesses in the barrio are auto repair shops, bakeries, small cafes, and <u>tortilla</u> factories. Tortillas are round, thin cornbread cakes.

In many cities, barrios have been torn down to make room for new housing projects, city buildings, or freeways. Then many families have to find new homes. As Mexican Americans have been able to earn more money in businesses and professional jobs, they have left the barrios. They have moved their families to areas with better housing and better services. In many cities, Mexican Americans are now living in all sections of town.

What are some problems that Mexican Americans face today?

The United States government has reported that almost one-third of the Mexican Americans do not earn enough in a year to give their families the housing, food, and clothing that they need. Unemployment among Mexican Americans is high. Some can find work only part of the year. Most of the jobs they have call for

As the amount of education a person has increases, so do his job possibilities.

unskilled manual labor and the pay is very low. Mexican Americans work at construction jobs, at making clothing, and taking care of buildings. Some work in offices and stores; others work in hotels, motels, and restaurants. Many work in farming jobs.

The lack of education is another serious problem among Mexican Americans. Many leave high school before they finish. In some states, at least one-fifth of the Mexican students drop out of high school before they graduate. In other states, still fewer finish school. Many Mexican Americans have a hard time learning English. They become discouraged, quit school, and go to work. Sometimes they have to get jobs to help their families.

What has the government done to help Mexican Americans?

Many Mexican Americans have served in the armed forces of the United States. The government has passed laws to help all veterans receive an education. Many Mexican American veterans are helped by those laws and they attend colleges and trade schools. Some have become teachers, doctors, lawyers, and accountants.

146

Members of our government have realized there are too many families living in poverty in the United States. Many of these families are Mexican Americans. Congress has passed laws to give them more educational and job opportunities.

One program to help young children is called Head Start. Children under six years old who need special help can begin school early. If they do not speak English, they can learn it in this program. It is hoped that because they get a "head start," they will do well in school.

Other programs were started by the Bilingual Education Act. Under this law, children can study in both English and Spanish. Educators believe that the Spanish-speaking children will learn English more quickly this way. They hope it will make them proud of their native language and their heritage. T.E.S.L. (Teaching English as a Second Language) is a popular program in some cities. Its purpose is to teach English as quickly as possible. Other programs help schools buy special books and materials to help all children learn.

To encourage high school students to go to college, many of them go to special college classes during the summer. Here they see what college life is like. It is hoped the students will decide to go to college when they finish high school.

Mexican American children learn English in school. This will help them all their lives.

This teacher with her classroom on wheels helps children learn English.

Another program is for young men who have quit school and do not want to go to college. Special schools give them training for jobs such as printers, auto mechanics, upholsterers, and electricians. The students also have classes in regular high school subjects. When they finish, they receive a high school diploma and a certificate to show that they have learned a trade.

There are also community programs to help end poverty and its causes. The programs have child day-care centers and hot lunches for old people. There are classes to teach adults how to read and write and how to become American citizens. One program has a Mobile Learning Laboratory. This is really a classroom on wheels which travels from one area of the city to another.

How are Mexican Americans overcoming some of their problems?

During the 1920's, some Mexican Americans in Texas formed an organization called the <u>Lulacs</u>. This stands for <u>League of United Latin American Citizens.</u> Today there are many Lulac clubs in the Southwest. They work for goodwill between the Anglo and Mexican American people. These clubs started preschool classes for Spanish-speaking children. The purpose was to teach them four hundred basic English words before they started school. These classes were the forerunners of the Head Start program.

Other organizations have been formed to involve Mexican Americans in social, political, and economic activities. Some of these groups have had demonstrations to point out the needs of Mexican Americans. Not all Mexican Americans agree with the aims of these groups. But they do show that Mexican Americans are learning to become politically and socially active.

There are also student groups at colleges and in some high schools. They want more courses taught about Mexican American history and culture. Throughout the state of Texas, courses such as these are part of the high school program.

These different groups have helped elect many city and county officials and school board members. They have also sent leaders to the state and national legislatures. Through these organizations, Mexican Americans can work to solve their problems.

What does the future hold for Mexican Americans?

Mexican Americans have had many of the same problems faced by other immigrants. Many are descendants of people living here when the Southwest joined the United States. But the great majority are truly immigrants. They came here mainly as unskilled laborers and contributed their hard work and knowledge of farming. This helped make the Southwest a great farming region.

These people are entering Texas from Mexico. The guard checks their papers to make sure they are correct.

The artist Manuel Acosta was born in Mexico, but lives in Texas. He helps enrich American life with his works.

"Portrait of Senora Concepcion S. Acosta" Courtesy of the artist

Now more farming is being done by machines, and the Southwest is building more industries. Farm workers have to find other kinds of jobs. Four out of five Mexican Americans now live in cities. Most of them are under 21 years of age. Many of them lack the skills and the education needed for jobs in industry.

Many Mexican Americans now believe that education is the best answer to their problems. They also believe that they must take a greater part in politics. They feel they must work to elect more Mexican Americans to government jobs. Ending discrimination in jobs and in other areas is another one of their goals.

Most Mexican Americans want to keep their heritage. They want their children to be proud of their language and culture. They are organizing theater groups to write and give plays about Mexican history and life. They are encouraging young artists and writers. They are proud to be Americans, but they are also proud to be Mexican Americans.

Who are some outstanding Mexican Americans?

Many Mexican Americans have served their country in war and peace. At least seventeen have won the Congressional Medal of

150

Standing from left to right are: Frank D. Veiga, President of the National Economic Development Association; Carlos Villarreal, Administrator of the Urban Mass Transportation Administration; Phillip Sanchez, Director, Office of Economic Opportunity; Robert Finch, Counsellor to the President; Romana Banuelos, Treasurer of The United States; Raymond Telles, United States Commissioner, Equal Employment Opportunity Commission; Henry Ramirez, Chairman, Cabinet Committee on Opportunities for The Spanish-speaking, Alfred R. Villalobos, Executive Vice President, National Economic Development Association.

Honor, the nation's highest military award for bravery in action. Raul R. Morin wrote a book, *Among the Valiant,* which describes their deeds. In honor of Morin's work to help Mexican Americans, Los Angeles established the "Raul Morin Memorial Square" in 1968.

Today in the Congress of the United States, several Mexican Americans contribute to the good of the nation. One of these is Congressman Edward R. Roybal of California, elected in 1962. Texas has two Mexican American Congressmen, Eligio de la Garza and Henry B. Gonzalez. De la Garza served six terms in the Texas legislature before becoming a United States representative. Gonzalez served in the Texas State Senate before his election to Congress. It had been 110 years since a Mexican American had served in the Texas Senate. New Mexico also has a Mexican American congressman. Manuel Lujan, Jr., was first elected in 1968 to the 91st Congress. He was re-elected to the 92nd Congress.

Joseph Montoya is greatly interested in conservation and also in the cultural heritage of the Southwest.

Joseph M. Montoya is a United States Senator from New Mexico. At 21, he was the youngest man ever elected to the New Mexico House of Representatives. He served as the state's lieutenant governor, and as a United States Congressman. He was appointed to the United States Senate to finish the term of another well-known Mexican American, Dennis Chavez. Montoya was re-elected in 1965 and has served ever since.

Other Mexican Americans are active in our government. Philip Sanchez of Chicago is the head of the U.S. Office of Economic Opportunity. Vincente Ximenes of Texas was Commissioner of the Equal Employment Opportunity Commission. He also served on the Inter-Agency Committee on Mexican-American Affairs.

Raymond L. Telles is from El Paso, Texas. He was an aide to Presidents Truman and Eisenhower when they visited Mexico. From 1957 to 1961 he served as Mayor of El Paso. He was also appointed by President Kennedy as Ambassador to Costa Rica, and held that post until 1967. Today he is Commissioner for the Equal Employment Opportunity Commission.

In education, there are many Mexican American leaders. For over forty years, Dr. George Sanchez has worked to improve the schools. He has tried to solve the social and educational problems of Mexican Americans. He is author of textbooks about Latin America. He takes part in many government conferences.

Dr. Julian Nava is a professor of history and a member of the Los Angeles City Board of Education. Armando Rodrigues, an immigrant from Mexico, has served as director of the Office for Spanish Speaking American Affairs in the United States Office of Education. He is now an assistant commissioner in the office. In 1971 one of the largest school systems in Texas, the El Paso Public Schools, created a division of Mexican American Education. Carlos Rivera, who has contributed greatly to education and to the teaching of Spanish, was made the assistant superintendent for the office. These people have all helped make better schools.

One of the best-known Mexican Americans is Caesar Chavez. He has worked many years to better the pay and working conditions of farm workers. He became the General Director of the Community Service Organization, which helped the workers start unions. He organized the National Farm Workers' Association (NFWA). As a result of a strike which he led, the NFWA and many of the grape growers of California have signed union contracts.

Mexican Americans have made names for themselves in other fields. Lee Trevino won three major golf tournaments in 1971. He was the champion of the United States, British, and Canadian Opens. For his outstanding achievements, sports writers voted him the Athlete of the Year for which he received the prized Hickok Belt. Richard Gonzalez, known as Poncho, is a great and famous tennis player.

Well-known in the field of business is Hilary Sandoval of El Paso, Texas. He was formerly head of the Small Business Administration in the United States government. Mrs. Ramona Banuelos of Los Angeles was appointed by President Nixon us the Treasurer of the United Slutes.

Ernesto Galarza was born in 1914 in Tepic, Nayarit, Mexico. He came to the United States when he was still a child. While he was young, Ernesto worked at many jobs. He was a farm laborer, a cannery worker, and even a court interpreter. For many years, while Mr. Galarza worked at these different jobs, he continued his education. He received his bachelor's and master's degrees and, finally, his doctorate, the highest degree possible.

Mr. Galarza followed many careers. He spent some years as a teacher, then he turned to writing. He wrote many books about the problems of Mexican immigrants, and his work in this field is very highly respected. Mr. Galarza was also active in labor and international positions. He served as the Director of Research and Education for the National Agricultural Workers Union. He was Chief of Labor and Social Information for the Pan American Union. Mr. Galarza was also an advisor to the Ford Foundation, the National Farmers Union, and the country of Bolivia.

Ernesto Galarza has worked to help many people. His hard work has especially helped his fellow Mexican Americans.

WHAT WOULD YOU DO?

Suppose you are Ernesto Galarza. You have worked hard to get your first college degree. You want to continue your education, but you must also work to earn your own living.

1. What are some jobs you might work at so you can go to school part-time?
2. What subjects will you be most interested in studying?
3. Why do you want to continue your education?
4. Will your education help you help your people? How?

WHAT DO YOU THINK?

1. List ten places of interest that have names of Spanish origin.
2. Explain why Mexican Americans are not always thought of as immigrants to this country.
3. Look at the map on page 141. Why were the Royal Roads important to the people?
4. Why do some Mexican Americans find life difficult in America?

5. Why did Spain and Mexico colonize the southwest at the time they did?
6. What can Anglos do to help Mexican Americans enjoy life in the United States?
7. Who are the chicanos? Why do you think they like to be called by that name?

8. Do you think other immigrants have the same problems Mexican Americans have when they come to this country? What problems do they have that are the same? What problems are different?
9. Why do you think more and more Mexican Americans are moving to large northern cities such as Detroit and Chicago?
10. In what ways have Mexican Americans contributed to our ideas of food and music?
11. The chart on page 133 shows how some Spanish and English words are much alike. Do you think learning Spanish would be easy? Why would it be good to know two languages?

This is a typical Puerto Rican-American family.

Other Hispano American Immigrants

Puerto Ricans come from a small island called Puerto Rico. The island is situated in the Caribbean Sea. It belongs to a group of islands called the Greater Antilles. The island was discovered by Christopher Columbus during his second trip to the New World in 1493.

Columbus took possession of the island in the name of the king and queen of Spain, Ferdinand and Isabella. Puerto Rico remained a Spanish colony until 1898.

Following the Spanish-American War in 1898, Spain gave the island to the United States in payment for American expenses during the war. The island remained a territory of the United States until 1952, when it became a *Commonwealth* with an association with the United States. This means that the Puerto Ricans make and enforce their own laws, so long as those laws are not harmful to the United States.

156

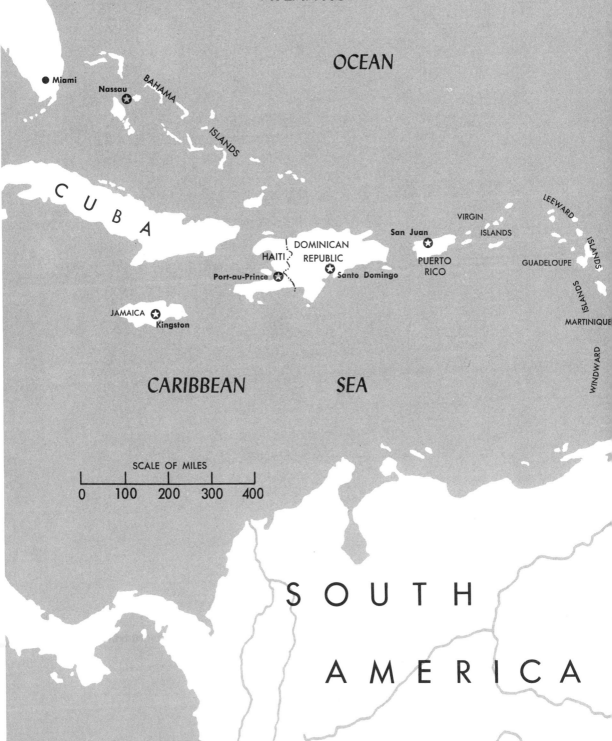

ATLANTIC

OCEAN

● Miami

Nassau ⭐

BAHAMA

ISLANDS

C U B A

LEEWARD

VIRGIN

San Juan ⭐

ISLANDS

ISLANDS

DOMINICAN
REPUBLIC

HAITI

PUERTO
RICO

GUADELOUPE

Port-au-Prince ⭐

Santo Domingo

ISLANDS

JAMAICA ⭐

MARTINIQUE

Kingston

CARIBBEAN   SEA

WINDWARD

SCALE OF MILES

0   100   200   300   400

S O U T H

A M E R I C A

Who are the Puerto Ricans?

Puerto Ricans cannot be considered immigrants when they come to the United States. They are in fact citizens of the United States. When they move to the mainland, it is very much like you and your family moving to another state. When you and your family move from one state to another, you are considered a <u>migrant</u>. Puerto Ricans are migrants.

But life in the United States is difficult for the Puerto Ricans. Imagine you and your family moved to a state where the people spoke a different language, ate different foods, and wore different clothes. It would not be easy for you. This is what happens to many Puerto Ricans when they come to the mainland.

In Puerto Rico, they speak Spanish, and learn to read and write Spanish in the schools. English is taught as an extra language. When they come to the United States many of them cannot speak English.

Their foods are different. Almost all Puerto Rican-American families have a mixture of beans and rice at every meal. It is a staple of their meals, just as potatoes are served with many meals in American families.

The Puerto Rican is used to a small town where everyone knows everyone else. When he comes to the mainland he often moves into the large cities where he may not know his next-door neighbor. The Puerto Rican is a friendly, warm person and the strangeness of a big city is often hard for him to adjust to. New families are glad if they can live near others like them, who enjoy the same kind of life.

Many Puerto Rican-Americans live in New York City.

Because the Puerto Ricans are American citizens, they can travel back and forth from the United States and Puerto Rico at will. They do not need to wait for quotas, as other newcomers to the United States do.

To travel from Puerto Rico to the United States is very much like traveling from New York to Chicago. The trip takes about two hours from San Juan, the capital of Puerto Rico, to Miami, Florida. It is about three and one half hours from San Juan to New York City and four and one half hours to Chicago, Illinois.

Puerto Rican-Americans often find it difficult to obtain work when they come to the United States.

In the picture above can be seen the work done by some of the people who came to the United States. Often women and children will help. It is hard work and the pay is low. These newcomers hope to have a better life someday.

Many of the Puerto Ricans come to work on the farms of the United States as migrant workers during the summer. This means that they come to the mainland for the summer season and return to the island until the next summer. But others decide to move to the large cities and look for industrial jobs.

Because the Puerto Ricans do not have skills in industrial work, the kind of work they find in the cities is not always well paid. This often forces them to live in the poorer neighborhoods of the large cities in crowded conditions.

160

Many Puerto Rican-Americans are forced to live in ghettos.

What are the problems of Puerto Rican-Americans?

Most of the Puerto Rican people who travel to the United States move into the big cities. Moreover, the life of the Puerto Ricans in our cities is often like that of the Afro-Americans. Both groups usually live in segregated areas that are made up of old, run-down houses and buildings. The Puerto Ricans often face injustice and low incomes. Their schools are sometimes poorer, too.

The life of the Puerto Rican-Americans is in some ways very different from the life of the Afro-Americans. For instance, when they arrive in the United States, they are already American citizens. Usually they speak only Spanish, so they have to learn English. They have strong ties to their native land.

One problem that Puerto Rican-Americans have in common with the Afro-Americans is that both must often have to rely on welfare and other social services. However, there are many groups in our cities, especially in New York City and Chicago, that are working to improve the lives of Puerto Rican-Americans. Many of these groups are Puerto Ricans themselves. These groups often help young and old with English, school work and in finding good jobs. They also organize book fairs, music and art shows.

Moreover, because religion is an important part of Puerto Rican life, churches and church groups can help in many ways. One basic way church groups try to help Puerto Rican newcomers is by helping them adjust to urban life. Moreover, cursillos—religious retreats —are often held for Puerto Ricans as a way of helping themselves.

Many Puerto Rican-Americans have come to the United States seeking a better way of life.

Some cities have parades in honor of various ethnic groups. Here Puerto Ricans are also honoring Christopher Columbus and his sailing ships. Why would they do this?

What does the future hold for Puerto Rican-Americans?

The future of Puerto Ricans in this nation, however, looks promising. This is true for several reasons. First, the many contributions that are being made in this nation by Puerto Rican individuals and groups are increasing. Large numbers of Puerto Rican-American businesses are also opening in cities such as New York City, Chicago, and Philadelphia. Moreover, many Puerto Rican-Americans are going to school, learning English, and going on to college and better jobs. Many also are beginning to adopt the customs and habits of the United States while still retaining the traditions and customs of Puerto Rico. Still others are working in government and becoming politically involved in the affairs of the United States. Thus, culturally, socially, economically and politically, Puerto Rican-Americans are becoming full-fledged Americans. And as the United States has welcomed and helped so many other people from other nations of the world we also welcome the Puerto Rican-American— our citizen immigrant.

What are Puerto Rican-American contributions to the United States?

Many Puerto Ricans have made great contributions to the United States. Teodoro Moscoso was the United States Ambassador to Venezuela. He was also the international director of the Alliance for Progress in Latin America. This is a program to help poor countries of Central and South America.

Jose A. Benitez and General Rivero have occupied high ranking positions in the United States' Army and Navy. The Puerto Ricans were a large contributor of soldiers to the United States Army during the Korean War. Thousands of young Puerto Ricans fought in the First and Second World Wars and in Vietnam.

Many Hispano-Americans must learn English when they come to the United States.

We Thank Congratulate Honor and Bless Fervently the Navy, Coast Guard, Customs and Immigration of U.S.A.
CUBAN REFUGEES

These Cuban refugees, already living in Florida, are shown waiting for more relatives and friends to arrive. They made this sign to express their thanks to the United States for welcoming them to America.

How have Cubans contributed to American life?

In 1959 Fidel Castro came to power in Cuba. Because he changed the government to a Communist dictatorship, many people were not happy. Thousands began to leave Cuba. Miami, Florida, became a refuge for these homeless people. Many of the Cubans had been highly-educated members of the middle- or upper-class. However, they spoke little or no English and had to leave their money and belongings in Cuba. Because of these things, the refugees had problems in America. They could get only low-paying jobs. They shined shoes, dug ditches, and washed dishes.

Today many of these same people have become wealthy owners of their own businesses. Others are presidents or vice presidents of banks. Some of Miami's finest restaurants are owned by Cuban-American citizens.

Jose O. Padron, a penniless Cuban refugee in 1962, has built his cigar manufacturing business into one of the biggest companies in Miami.

These successful Cubans are proud of their old culture. They work to preserve it so their children and grandchildren will learn how life in Cuba used to be. There are Cuban schools and hospitals. There is a sports club fashioned after those that used to be in Havana, the capital of Cuba.

The Cuban-Americans are now fairly settled socially and economically. They have time to become more interested in their local government. Some people think Miami will have a Cuban mayor by 1975. There are about 350,000 Cubans in the Miami area. They make up one-fourth of the population there. These former refugees are now highly-respected citizens. They have contributed greatly to the economy of Florida.

WHAT DO YOU THINK?

1. Find Puerto Rico on the map on page 157.
2. What language problem do Puerto Ricans have when they migrate to America?
3. Why did so many Cubans come to the United States?

4. How did the United States gain Puerto Rico?
5. In what ways is life here different from life in Puerto Rico?
6. How does the church help Puerto Rican immigrants?

7. What is a commonwealth?
8. What is the difference between a migrant and an immigrant?
9. What is the work of the Alliance for Progress?
10. How do you think Cubans have contributed to American life?

Today's Immigrants

How have the numbers of immigrants changed?

The chart below shows some interesting facts. For instance, if you look down the Eastern Europe column you will see that in 1900, more than 97,000 people came to America. But in 1950, only about 800 came. Do you know why? What reasons can you name for this happening?

Another interesting column is the one for the Americas. See how the number has jumped to almost four times what it was in 1950. More than 44,000 of these people were from Mexico. This column also includes Canada and South America. Can you discover other events in history that were responsible for larger or smaller numbers of immigrants coming to America?

IMMIGRATION TO THE UNITED STATES

Year	Northwestern Europe	Central Europe	Eastern Europe	Southern Europe	Asia	Americas	Australia	Totals
1850	228,148	78,901	46	1,228	7	15,768	0	324,098
1900	85,212	133,354	97,639	108,495	17,946	5,455	428	448,529
1920	85,997	11,480	5,664	143,154	17,505	90,025	2,185	356,010
1950	35,115	147,080	803	16,111	3,779	44,191	517	247,596
1970	24,457	22,508	2,089	60,325	89,720	161,727	2,693	263,519
Totals	258,929	393,323	106,241	329,313	128,957	317,166	5,823	

America's most recent immigrants are from Cuba. Many Cubans have come to the United States to escape from the present government of Cuba.

Who are today's immigrants?

The immigration laws of 1965 ended the quotas that for forty years kept many immigrants from coming to the United States. Now larger numbers of immigrants from southern and eastern Europe, Asia, and Africa may come to our country.

In the days of the great waves of immigration, people moved westward to find more room on the frontier. Today Americans are still on the move. They are moving from place to place within the United States. Thousands of southern Negroes and whites are moving to the North. Many people are moving from small towns into cities. In the cities, people are moving from neighborhood to neighborhood as old homes are being torn down to make room for new ones. Many other people are moving from the city to the suburbs. People retire and move to Florida or California.

The areas outside cities were mostly vacant a few years ago. Today, these communities have rows and rows of new houses. Many neighborhoods now have a wide variety of people from many different nationality, religious, and racial backgrounds. Other neighborhoods have the same kind of people living in them.

169

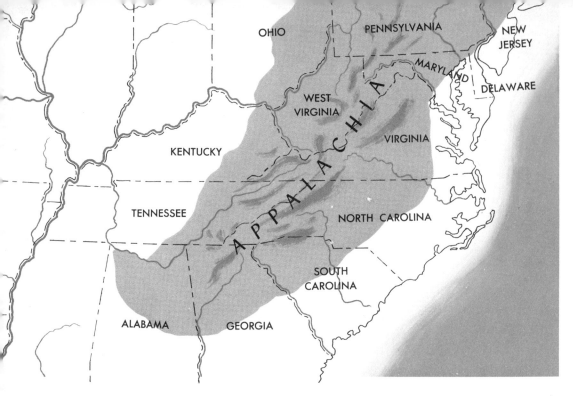

Most of today's newcomers to the cities are blacks, Mexicans, Puerto Ricans, American Indians, and people from the Appalachian Mountain region. Like the immigrants of long ago, they are looking for jobs and a better life for their families. In many ways they are having a harder time than the early immigrant Poles, Irish, or Germans. Many of today's migrants have been in the United States for several generations, but they are strangers to the large cities. A big adjustment in their lives is necessary.

Many of the immigrants who came to the United States in the early twentieth century did not speak English, but they could find work in laboring jobs. They were able to work on canals and railroads and in mines. Now jobs have changed. There is less need for heavy labor. Machines do most of the work. There are no peddlers. Supermarkets take care of the household needs. Today's newcomers find it hard to get jobs in cities. Many Puerto Ricans and Mexicans speak little English, which causes added problems in getting jobs. The blacks may meet the problem of racial prejudice when they look for a place to live. Although Indians and white Appalachians speak English, their dialects, or regional speech, and their customs are different from other Americans. Most have problems of poverty, lack of education, and the feeling of being rejected by many of their new neighbors.

The old immigrants needed us, and we needed them. Over-population was not a problem. Now there are too many people for the jobs available in large cities. Many migrants are added to welfare rolls. They must crowd into slum housing that is available at low cost. The overcrowded schools and hospitals cannot take care of all the newcomers.

City and community agencies have programs to help these new-comers adjust to city living. But often there is not enough money to provide all the help that is needed.

The Polish, Czech, and other immigrant groups could save some of their pay and eventually buy a house. Today the cost of land and taxes is very high. For many of these newcomers there is little chance of owning their own home. Most of them are thankful if they earn enough money for food and shelter. Housing built with government financing is one source of hope for those who wish to own property. Rehabilitation of old houses is also a way for some newcomers to have better housing.

Community, city, state, and federal government leaders are trying to find ways to help today's newcomers and also to improve the big cities. Local school councils in cities meet to talk about ways to improve the schools. Parents, community leaders, and teachers work together on special needs of the community and of the schools.

President and Mrs. Nixon are shown here at a reception for new citizens. These immigrants represent countries from many parts of the world.

The federal government is working with many of the big city governments to help rebuild some inner-city communities. This is called the Model Cities Program. This program helps cities get new buildings for homes and schools. It helps people learn the things they need to know to live and work in the city. It tries to provide more jobs for poor people and it offers better health service. The Model Cities Program and the other government programs have not solved all the urban problems. But this is a good beginning. There is hope for all newcomers that they, too, will find the better life that many early immigrant families found in the new world after many years.

What is life like for our modern American Indians?

The American Indians have been called our country's first citizens. They have lived here longer than anyone else and have lived mainly as farmers and hunters.

When explorers and settlers came to America, the Indians were afraid their land would be taken from them. Over the years, this has happened. Today's Indians, if they live on a government reservation, find life very poor. Regulations have limited their rights to fish and hunt. Land that belonged to them by treaty, or agreement, has been sold to others. Schools do not have the things necessary to do a good job of teaching. Many students drop out of school too early in life and remain unable to read and write English. About 35,000 children are sent hundreds of miles from home to boarding schools owned by the government. They may not see their families for a whole year.

Some Indians have moved to large cities. Because most of them are not well-educated, it is very hard to find good jobs. Most of them face an unhappy future. Robert Bennett, an Indian himself, was Commissioner of the Bureau of Indian Affairs. It is a part of our federal government. He hopes that more Americans will become interested in helping our first citizens.

A declaration, or statement, made by Cherokee Indians long ago said, in part:

"In these days, we are losing our homes and our children's homes. When our homeland is protected, for ourselves and for the generations to follow, we shall rest.

"In the vision of our creator, we declare ourselves ready to stand proudly among the nationalities of these United States of America."

173

The Statue of Liberty was given to the United States by France. It is the symbol of our freedom. A Spanish Jew, Emma Lazarus, wrote the beautiful and inspiring words:

"Give me your tired, your poor,
your huddled masses yearning to breathe free,
The wretched refuse of your teeming shore.
Send these, the homeless, tempest-tost to me,
I lift the lamp beside the golden door!"

Through the years, people came to America for many reasons. Some came for political freedom, some for religious freedom, and some for adventure. America offered and will continue to offer the promise of a better life, hope, and freedom to all people that come to her shores.

Emma Lazarus wrote the poem that is on the Statue of Liberty. The poem is called "The New Colossus."

We are living up to democratic American principles

IF we judge each person on his own accord.

IF we try to have friends among people of various racial,
nationality, and religious groups.

IF we refuse to listen to rumors and gossip about whole
groups of people.

IF we recognize that Americans of all races, creeds, and
nationalities have helped build our country and made
it free and prosperous.

IF we insist that all Americans have the same rights we
insist on for ourselves.

IF we work for good jobs, good schools, and good homes
for everybody.

by Willard Johnson
Former National Program Director
National Conference of Christians and Jews

Any immigrant who fulfills the requirements for becoming a citizen of the United States must take this <u>oath,</u> or promise.

OATH OF ALLEGIANCE

I hereby declare, on oath, that I absolutely and entirely renounce and abjure all allegiance and fidelity to any foreign prince, potentate, state or sovereignty, of whom or which I have heretofore been a subject or citizen; that I will support and defend the Constitution and laws of the United States of America against all enemies, foreign and domestic; that I will bear true faith and allegiance to the same; that I will bear arms on behalf of the United States when required by the law; that I will perform non-combatant service in the armed forces of the United States when required by the law; that I will perform work of national importance under civilian direction when required by the law, and that I take this obligation freely without any mental reservations or purpose of evasion; so help me God.

WHAT DO YOU THINK?

1. Why is "nation of immigrants" a good name for America?
2. When Americans travel abroad, why should they use their very best manners? Why would noisy behavior, careless dress, and poor manners hurt America?
3. Why are you proud to be an American? How can you show your love for America?

4. What holidays are celebrated by certain nationalities?
5. What holidays are typically American?
6. How do the newcomers to the cities today differ from the immigrants of the 1890's?
7. Why is education and vocational training even more important to newcomers today than it was seventy-five years ago?

8. What kind of government help is there for newcomers today that was not available in 1900?
9. Which groups of people are considered minority groups today?
10. Were some European immigrant groups once considered minority groups in America? Explain.
11. Why do American Indians and Appalachian Whites often have a hard time in the cities today?
12. What do you think the words on the Statue of Liberty mean?
". . .Give me your tired, your poor,
Your huddled masses yearning to breathe free. . ."

Louis Adamic
Yugoslavia
Writer

Louis Agassiz
Switzerland
Naturalist

Spiro Agnew
Greece
Vice-President

Sholom Aleichem
Jewish
Writer

Ernst F. W. Alexanderson
Swedish
Engineer, Inventor

Marian Anderson
Africa
Concert Singer

Crispus Attucks
Africa
Patriot

John J. Audubon
France
Ornithologist

Benjamin Banneker
Africa
Mathematician

Ramona Banuelos
Mexico
United States Treasurer

Alexander G. Bell
Scotland
Inventor

Vincent Bendix
Sweden
Inventor

Jose A. Benitez
Puerto Rico
Army Officer

Jack Benny
Jewish
Entertainer

Mary McLeod Bethune
Africa
Educator

Edward Bok
The Netherlands
Journalist

Louis B. Brandeis
Jewish
Supreme Court Justice

Edward Brooke
Africa
United States Senator

Gwendolyn Brooks
Africa
Poet

Constantino Brumidi
Italy
Artist

Ralph J. Bunche
Africa
Diplomat

Mother Francis Cabrini
Italy
Roman Catholic Nun

Cleofante Campanini
Italy
Musician

Benjamin Cardozo
Jewish
Supreme Court Justice

Andrew Carnegie
Scotland
Industrialist

Jose Carrillo
Mexico
Politician

Enrico Caruso
Italy
Opera Singer

George Washington Carver
Africa
Scientist, Teacher

Caesar Chavez
Mexico
Labor Leader

Edward Corsi
Italy
Commissioner of Immigration

Lilly Dache
France
Milliner, Designer

Leopold Damrosch
Germany
Musician

Walter Damrosch
Germany
Musician

Lorenzo Delmonico
Switzerland
Restaurateur

Joe DiMaggio
Italy
Baseball Player

Manuel Dominguez
Mexico
Politician

Frederick A. Douglass
Africa
Leader, Abolition Movement

W.E.B. DuBois
Africa
Writer

Jean Pointe DuSable
Africa
Settler, Trader

Albert Einstein
Germany
Physicist

Dwight D. Eisenhower
Germany
General and 34th President

Mischa Elman
Russia
Musician

John Ericsson
Sweden
Inventor, Engineer

Pierre Faneuil
France
Merchant

Stephen Foster
Scotch-Irish
Composer

Felix Frankfurter
Jewish
Supreme Court Justice

Rudolf Friml
Czechoslovakia
Musician

Casimir Funk
Poland
Biochemist

Albert Gallatin
Switzerland
Secretary of State

Eligio de la Garza
Mexico
United States Congressman

George Gershwin
Jewish
Composer

Amadeo Giannini
Italy
Banker

Richard Gonzales
Mexico
Tennis Champion

Henry B. Gonzalez
Mexico
United States Congressman

William R. Grace
Ireland
Mayor of New York City

Pablo de la Guerra
Mexico
Politician

Oscar Hammerstein
Jewish
Businessman, Philanthropist

Oscar Hammerstein II
Jewish
Composer

S. I. Hayakawa
Japan
Teacher, Writer

Jasha Heifetz
Russia
Musician

Victor Herbert
Ireland
Composer

Herbert Hoover
German
31st President

Vladimir Horowitz
Russia
Musician

Ales Hrdlicka
Czechoslovakia
Anthropologist

Thomas Hum
China
Doctor

Daniel K. Inouye
Japan
Senator

Lyman Jee
China
Architect, Land Developer

Elia Kazan
Greece
Writer, Movie Director

John F. Kennedy
Ireland
35th President

Martin Luther King
Africa
Civil Rights Leader

Father Eusebio Kino
Spain
Missionary

Emil Konopinski
Poland
Physicist

Zdenek Kopal
Czechoslovakia
Astronomer

Dragos D. Kostich
Yugoslavia
Teacher, Newscaster

Fiorello LaGuardia
Italy
Mayor of New York City

179

Wanda Landowska
Poland
Musician

Mario Lanza
Italy
Singer

Benjamin Latrobe
England
Architect

Emma Lazarus
Jewish
Poet

T. D. Lee
China
Physicist

Pierre Charles L'Enfant
France
Engineer, City Planner

Charles Lindbergh, Jr.
Sweden
Airplane Pilot

Charles Lindbergh, Sr.
Sweden
Lawyer, Congressman

Sinclair Louie
China
Merchant

Ah Louis
China
Merchant

Manuel Lujan, Jr.
Mexico
United States Congressman

John McCormack
Ireland
Singer

Rocky Marciano
Italy
Heavyweight Boxer

Thurgood Marshall
Africa
U. S. Supreme Court

Giovanni Martinelli
Italy
Opera Singer

Masayuki Matsunaga
Japan
United States Congressman

George Meany
Ireland
Labor Leader

C. E. Kenneth Mees
England
Photographic Researcher

Albert Michelson
Germany
Physicist

Arthur Miller
Jewish
Writer

Nathan Milstein
Russia
Musician

John Mitchell
Ireland
Labor Leader

Dimitri Mitropoulos
Greece
Conductor, Musician

Helena Modjeska
Poland
Actress

Ralph Modjeski
Poland
Engineer

Joseph M. Montoya
Mexico
United States Senator

Raul R. Morin
Mexico
Writer

Mary Mortimer
England
Teacher

Teodoro Moscoso
Puerto Rico
United States Ambassador

Stan Musial
Poland
Baseball Player

Edmund Muskie
Poland
Governor, U. S. Senator

Julian Nava
Mexico
Teacher and Writer

Jose Navarro
Mexico
State Senator

Hideyo Noguchi
Japan
Doctor, Medical Researcher

Frederick Novy
Czechoslovakia
Bacteriologist

Milton L. Olive III
Africa
Viet Nam Soldier

Don Juan de Onate
Spain
Explorer

Eugene O'Neill
Ireland
Writer

Thomas Paine
England
Writer and Statesman

George Papanicolaou
Greece
Doctor, Medical Researcher

Joe Pepitone
Italy
Baseball Player

John J. Pershing
Germany
World War I General

Attilio Piccirilli
Italy
Sculptor

George Placzek
Czechoslovakia
Physicist

Albin Polasek
Czechoslovakia
Sculptor

Lily Pons
France
Opera Singer

Leontyne Price
Africa
Opera Singer

Casimir Pulaski
Poland
Soldier

Joseph Pulitzer
Hungary
Journalist

Michael Pupin
Yugoslavia
Physicist

Paul Revere
France
Patriot, Silversmith

Jacob Riis
Denmark
Social Worker

Carlos Rivera
Mexico
Teacher

Phil Rizzuto
Italy
Baseball Player

Knute Rockne
Norway
Football Coach

Armando Rodrigues
Mexico
U. S. Office of Education

Artur Rodzinski
Poland
Musician

John Augustus Roebling
Germany
Engineer

Ole Rolvaag
Norway
Teacher, Writer

Franklin D. Roosevelt
The Netherlands
32nd President

Theodore Roosevelt
The Netherlands
26th President

Edward R. Roybal
Mexico
United States Senator

Jose Ruiz
Mexico
Politician

Augustus Saint-Gaudens
Ireland
Artist, Sculptor

Peter Salem
Africa
Revolutionary War Soldier

Antonio Salemme
Italy
Sculptor

Jonas Salk
Jewish
Doctor, Medical Researcher

George Sanchez
Mexico
Teacher, Writer

Philip Sanchez
Mexico
Government Official

Hilary Sandoval
Mexico
Businessman

Carl Schurz
Germany
Politician

Rudolf Serkin
Czechoslovakia
Concert Pianist

Father Junipero Serra
Spain
Missionary

Anna Howard Shaw
England
Doctor, Minister, Suffragette

William Shockley
England
Scientist

Igor Sikorsky
Russia
Aeronautical Engineer

Skouras Brothers
Greece
Movie Studio Owners

Al Smith
Ireland
Governor of New York

James Smith
Ireland
Lawyer and Judge

Haym Solomon
Jewish
Revolutionary War Patriot

Charles Steinmetz
Germany
Electrical Engineer

Leopold Stokowski
Poland
Musician

Igor Stravinsky
Russia
Musician

Gilbert Stuart
Scotland
Artist

Peter Stuyvesant
The Netherlands
Early Governor

Louis H. Sullivan
Ireland
Architect

John Sutter
Switzerland
Pioneer Settler

Henry O. Tanner
Africa
Artist

George Taylor
Ireland
Statesman

Edward Teller
Hungary
Physicist

Raymond L. Telles
Mexico
Mayor, Ambassador, Official

Nikola Tesla
Austria
Inventor

Matthew Thornton
Ireland
Statesman

Arturo Toscanini
Italy
Musician, Conductor

Lee Trevino
Mexico
Golf Champion

Oscar Tschirky
Switzerland
Chef

Richard Upjohn
England
Architect

Mariano Vallejo
Mexico
General and U. S. Senator

Martin Van Buren
The Netherlands
8th President

Carl Van Doren
The Netherlands
Writer

Mark Van Doren
The Netherlands
Writer

Hendrik Van Loon
The Netherlands
Writer

Calvert Vaux
England
Architect

Francis Vigo
Italy
Explorer, Army Colonel

Dr. Wernher Von Braun
Germany
Scientist

Lillian Wald
Jewish
Public Health Nurse

Booker T. Washington
Africa
Educator

Robert Weaver
Africa
Cabinet Member

Roy Wilkins
Africa
Civil Rights Leader

C. S. Wu
China
Physicist

Vincente Ximenes
Mexico
Government Official

Minour Yamasaki
Japan
Architect

C. N. Yang
China
Physicist

Carl Yastrzemski
Poland
Baseball Player

Whitney M. Young
Africa
Civil Rights Leader

Lorenzo de Zavela
Mexico
Vice-President of Texas

John Zeleny
Czechoslovakia
Physicist

Summary of Basic Concepts

America has welcomed the poor and homeless immigrants of the world. These people have made America one of the greatest nations in the world.

The United States of America is a nation of immigrants. Pages: 7-9, 23-25, 31, 62, 98, 113, 117, 122, 124, 168.

There were no original Americans. The Indians came from Asia. The first voyages of discovery were made by the Scandinavian Vikings. Columbus, an Italian, sailed to the New World for Spain. Later, the English, French, and Dutch came to America. Slaves were brought from Africa. People of many nations came to America. The ancestors of all Americans came from other countries. The heritage of America comes from immigrants who settled and built the nation.

Almost every group and nationality in the world is represented in the United States of America. Pages: 10-13, 23-25, 29-31, 62, 69, 98, 169.

Waves of immigrants came to America. The first wave was the English and other western European peoples. Slave ships came to America bringing Africans. People from northern Europe emigrated. Later people from southern and eastern Europe emigrated. The last great wave came after World War II. The people came from all corners of the earth: Asia, Europe, Africa, and South America.

The immigrants faced many hardships when they came to the United States. Pages: 15-16, 22, 27, 98-100, 124.

People in Europe had heard that the streets were paved with gold in America. But they found this was not true. The immigrants faced unemployment, low-paying jobs, living in ghettos, and discrimination.

There were many advantages in the United States that were not in the countries from which the immigrants came. Pages: 14, 21, 35, 113, 117, 124, 174.

To escape war, starvation, and hatred in the old country, people emigrated to America. In America, people were far from European wars and there was no starvation. There was also freedom of religion and political freedom.

All groups have contributed to the richness and variety of American life and American culture. Pages: 18-20, 26, 34, 36, 42, 46, 49, 52, 55, 62, 71, 75, 78, 86, 89, 92, 98, 113, 117, 122, 124, 131, 156, 168.

All fields of study have been enriched by the contributions of people of various immigrant groups. Entertainment, drama, art, and music have been created by people from many countries. The sciences, technology, law, government, and education have been influenced and enriched by the discoveries of immigrants or their descendants.

Pronunciation Symbols

By permission. From Webster's Seventh New Collegiate Dictionary, copyright 1971 by G. & C. Merriam Company, publishers of the Merriam-Webster Dictionaries.

a as in map	i as in tip	s as in less
ā as in day	ī as in side	sh as in shy
ä as in cot	j as in job	t as in tie
à as in father	k as in kin	th as in thin
aù as in out	l as in pool	th as in then
b as in baby	m as in dim	ū as in rule
ch as in chin	n as in no	ù as in pull
d as in did	ŋ as in sing	v as in give
e as in bed	ō as in bone	w as in we
ē as in easy	ò as in saw	y as in yard
f as in cuff	òi as in coin	z as in zone
g as in go	p as in lip	zh as in vision
h as in hat	r as in rarity	ə as in banana, collect

Glossary

The words pronounced and defined below are those words underlined and defined in the text. The numbers indicate the pages on which the words are first defined.

Abolition Movement /ˌab-ə-'lish-ən 'müv-mənt/ The attempt to stop slavery. 102

acequia /ə-'sā-kē-ə/ A canal for irrigation. 138

adobe /ə-'dō-bē/ A mixture of clay, soil, and straw for making bricks for Indian pueblos. 139

almanac /'òl-mə-ˌnak/ A book of facts about the days, months, sun, and moon. 105

Anglo /ˌaŋ-(ˌ)glō/ A white American. 142

anthropologist /ˌan(t)-thrə-'päl-ə-jəst/ A scientist who studies the beginnings of man. 7

arroyo /ə-'ròi-ə/ A large, dry gully formed by water. 133

barrio /'bahr-ree-oh/ A Mexican American neighborhood. 144

batea /bah-'te-ah/ A wooden bowl used in placer mining. 140

bonanza /bə-'nan-zə/ A gold or silver strike. 140

botas /'bōh-taz/ High-heeled boots for horseback riding. 139

Camino Real /Cah-'mee-no Re-'ahl/ A royal road or highway. 141

carillon /'kar-ə-ˌlän/ A tower with bells in it. 54

census /'sen(t)-səs/ An official counting of people. 13

chaparral /ˌshap-ə-'ral/ Brush country. 139

chapparreras /chah-pahr-'re-rahs/ Leather chaps for protecting the legs. 139

charter /'chärt-ər/ Written permission to settle the land. 10

chicano /chee-'kah-nō/ A name for a Mexican American. 131

churro /'chur-roh/ A scrubby but hardy sheep. 140

civil right /'siv-əl 'rīt/ The right of personal liberty guaranteed to American citizens. 109

colonia /cō-'lō-nee-ah/ A rural Mexican American settlement. 144

commonwealth /'käm-ən-,welth/ A land which makes its own laws, but is united with another land. 156

continent /'känt-ən-ənt/ A great area of land. 7

convert /kən-'vərt/ To make Christian. 135

craftsman /'kraf(t)-smən/ One who is a skilled worker. 57

culture /'kəl-chər/ The customs, traditions, and habits of people. 6

curio shop /'kyùr-ē-,ō 'shäp/ A store that sells unusual things. 116

declaration /,dek-lə-'rā-shən/ A statement or announcement made by one person to another. 173

dialect /'dī-ə-,lekt/ A difference in speech found in various parts of the country. 171

El Mar Pacifico /El Mahr Pah-'see-fee-cō/ The Pacific Ocean, or peaceful sea. 133

Emancipation Proclamation /i ,man(t)-sə-'pa-shən präk-lə-'mā-shən/ The document that gave freedom to the slaves. 104

glee club /'glē 'kləb/ A group of people who sing together. 58

homestead right /'hōm-sted 'rīt/ A law giving land to the people who settle it. 21

indentured servant /in-'den-chərd 'sər-vənt/ A person who works for someone else to repay money. 36

Industrial Revolution /in-'dəs-tre-əl rev-ə-'lü-shən/ The time when machines for manufacturing were first used. 14

irrigation /,ir-ə-'gā-shən/ The watering of dry land. 138

La reata /lah re-'ah-tah/ A lasso for catching cattle. 140

Los Primeros /lōs pree-'meh-rōs/ The first settlers in the Southwest. 133

Lulac /lü'lak/ The League of United Latin American Citizens. 148

lullaby /'ləl-ə-,bī/ A song for young children. 125

madre /'mah-dre/ Mother. 138

majority /mə-'jòr-ət-ē/ The larger part of a group. 107

mazurka /mə-'zər-kə/ A Slovak dance. 19

mesa /'mā-sə/ A flat-topped mountain. 133

migration /mī-'grā-shən/ Movement to another land. 10

milliner /'mil-ə-nər/ A person who makes hats. 48

minority /mə-'nȯr-ət-ē/ The smaller part of a group. 107

missionary /'mish-ə-,ner-ē/ A priest or minister of a church. 134

nationality /,nash-(ə)-'nal-ət-ē/ A feeling of belonging to a certain nation. 13

nisei /(')nē-'sā/ People born in America whose parents were born in Japan. 117

oath /'ōth/ A promise. 176

operetta /'äp-ə-'ret-ə/ A short opera with gay music. 39

pastor /pahs-'tohr/ A person who herds sheep. 140

placer mining /'plas-ər 'mī-ni ŋ/ A kind of gold mining. 140

polka /'pōl-kə/ A slovak dance. 19

Potato Blight /pə-'tāt-(,)ō 'blīt/ A disease which can kill potato plants. 14

presidio /pri-'sēd-ē-,ō/ A small fort. 135

pueblo /pü-'eb-(,)lō/ A town in the Southwest. 134

queue /'kyü/ A long pigtail worn by some Chinese years ago. 114

quota /'kwōt-ə/ A limit on numbers of new immigrants. 30

ranchero /ran-'che(ə)r(,)ō/ A rancher. 140

rancho /'ran-(,)chō/ A ranch. 140

refugee /ref-yu̇-'jē/ One who goes to another country for safety. 25

rodeo /'rōd-ē-,ō/ A roundup of cattle. 140

saga /'säg-ə/ A story of a historic hero. 8

slave /'slāv/ A person bought or sold by others. 99

smorgasbord /'smȯr-gəs-bȯ(ə)rd/ A meal with many kinds of food, which is a custom in Sweden. 65

Sokol /'sō-kəl/ A group that does gymnastics. 86

sombrero /səm-'bre(ə)r-(,)ō/ A large-brimmed hat. 139

steerage /'sti(ə)r-ij/ A place below decks on a ship. 15

substance /'səb-stən(t)s/ The important part of something. 82

synagogue /'sin-i-,gäg/ A Jewish house of worship. 124

theory /'thē-ə-rē/ An idea or explanation. 61

tienda /tee-'en-dah/ A Mexican American grocery store. 145

tortilla /tȯr-'tē-(y)ə/ A round, thin cornbread cake. 145

tradition /trə-'dish-ən/ A custom or habit of a group of people. 12

treaty /'trēt-ē/ An agreement or contract in writing between two states or peoples. 173

Underground Railroad /ən-dər-'graủnd 'ra(ə)l-,rōd/ An escape route for slaves 102

vaquero /vä-'ke(ə)r-(,)ō/ A Mexican cowboy. 139

Index

Words shown here in bold face type will also be found in the Glossary, where the definition and pronunciation are given.

Iceland, 8
indentured servants, 36, 78, 99
Independence Hall, 173
Indians, 7, 8, 101, 131, 132, 135, 136, 138, 140, 170, 171, 173
Industrial Revolution, 14
Inouye, Daniel K., 120
Inter-Agency Committee on Mexican-American Affairs, 152
Irish immigrants, 11, 13, 23, 24, 36-41, 70, 108
irrigation, 138, 142
Isabella of Spain, 156
Italians, 19, 69, 71-77, 108

Jamestown, 99
Japanese American Citizens League, 118
Japanese immigrants, 24, 117-121
Jee, Lyman, 116
Jefferson, Thomas, 43, 49
Jewish immigrants, 9, 24, 124-129
Johnson, Lyndon B., 32, 109
Johnson, Willard, 175

Kazan, Elia, 93
Kennedy, John F., 32, 40, 109, 152
kindergarten, 58
King, Martin Luther, Jr., 110
Kino, Father Eusebio, 136
Know-Nothings, 27
Kodak Research Laboratories, 43
Konopinski, Emil, 82
Kopal, Zdenek, 87
Korean War, 164
Kosciuszko, Tadeusz, 78
Kostich, Dragos D., 96
Kovarik, Alois, 87

Ladies Home Journal, 54
Lafayette, Marquis de, 46
La Garza, Eligio de, 151
La Guardia, Fiorello, 76
La Guerra, Pablo de, 141
Landowska, Wanda, 82
Lanza, Mario, 75
La reata, 140
La Rosa Macaroni Company, 75
Latrobe, Benjamin, 44
Lazarus, Emma, 128, 173
League of United Latin American Citizens (Lulacs), 148
Lee, T. D., 116
L'Enfant, Pierre Charles, 46
Lincoln, Abraham, 104
Lincoln Center, 106
Lindbergh, Charles A., Jr., 66
Lindbergh, Charles A., Sr., 66
Lithuania, 81
"Little Italy", 72, 108
Los Primeros, 133
Louie, Sinclair, 116
Lujan, Manuel Jr., 151
Lulacs, see League of United Latin American Citizens
lullaby, 125

McCormack, John, 40
Madison, James, 49

madre, 138
Maine Memorial, 74
majority, 107
Manhattan Island, 52
Marciano, Rocky, 76
Marshall, Thurgood, 107
Martin, Dean, 76
Martinelli, Giovanni, 75
Masaryk, Tomas, 88
Matagordo Bay, 133
Matsunaga, Masayuki, 120
Mayor of Chicago, 88
Mayor of El Paso, 152
Mayor of New York, 38, 76
mazurka, 19
Meany, George, 38
Mees, C. E. Kenneth, 43
mesa, 133
Metropolitan Museum of Art, 44
Metropolitan Opera Company, 40, 47, 75, 93, 106
Metropolitan Opera House, 75, 106
Mexican Americans, 24, 131-153, 170
Mexican War, 137, 142
Mexico City, 134, 135
Michelson, Albert, 59
migrant, 158
migration, 10
Miller, Arthur, 128
milliner, 48
Milstein, Nathan, 90
Milwaukee Female College, 44
minority, 107
Minuit, Peter, 62
missionary, 134-136
missions, 135, 136
Missouri River, 49
Mitchell, John, 37, 41
Mitropoulos, Dimitri, 93
Mobile Learning Laboratory, 148
Model Cities Program, 172
Modjeska, Helena, 82
Modjeski, Ralph, 83
Molly Maguires, 37
Monitor, The 65
Montoya, Joseph M., 152
Moravia, 84, 85
Morin, Raul R., 151
Mortimer, Mary, 44
Moscoso, Teodoro, 164
motto, United States, 173
Mulberry Street, 72
Museum of Natural History, 44
Musial, Stan, 82
Muskie, Edmund, 82
"My Old Kentucky Home", 43
"My Wild Irish Rose", 40

National Academy of Science, 50
National Association For the Advancement of Colored People (NAACP), 107
National Audubon Society, 47
National Baseball Hall of Fame, 76
National Conference of Christians and Jews, 175
National Farm Workers' Association (NFWA), 153
National Origin Act, 1924, 31

ACKNOWLEDGEMENTS

Our thanks to the following for permission to reproduce the photographs in this book.

Acosta, Manuel, 150

American Foundation, The, 54

Architect of the Capitol, 74

Balzekas Museum of Lithuanian Culture, Chicago, 81

Bettman Archive, Inc., The, 42, 52, 104, 126, 137

Boston Chamber of Commerce, 46

Bowdoin College Museum of Art, Brunswick, Maine, 43

Brown Brothers, 59

California Department of Public Works, 83

California Historical Society, 136, 138

Chicago Historical Society, 22 (bottom), 70, 72, 80

Chicago Park District, 88

Chinese American Civic Council, Chicago, 116

Columbia University, 95

Culver Pictures, Inc., 113

David, Sargon, 123

Denver Public Library, Western Collection, 140

Department of Justice, Immigration and Naturalization Service, 149

E. I. DuPont de Nemours and Company, 47 (left)

El Paso Public Schools, 147

Fujihirg, 161, 162, 164

George Eastman House, 16

Gorecki Studios, 19, 39

Hartmann, Clifford, 131

Historical Pictures Service, Chicago, 143

Holland Tulip Time Festival, Inc., 53

Hull House Association, 22 (top)

Jacobson, Selma, 64

Japanese National Tourist Organization, 119

Library of Congress, 37, 38, 44, 50, 61, 79, 174 (right)

Courtesy of Little Norway, Blue Mounds, Wisconsin, 62, 63, 66

Marshall Field & Co., 56

Metropolitan Opera Association, 106

Millard Tschudy Collection, 49

Courtesy Senator Joseph Montoya, 152

Museum of the City of New York, 174

NAACP, 109

NASA, 60

National Audubon Society, 47 (right)

National Carl Schurz Association, Inc., 55, 58

National Economic Development Association, 151

New York Convention and Visitors Bureau, 159

New York Public Library, Theater Collection, 40, 57

Courtesy Northwestern National Life Insurance Company, Minneapolis, Minn., 120

Courtesy Jose O. Padron, 166

Photography Unlimited, Westchester, Ill., 84, 93, 131

San Francisco Convention and Visitors Bureau, 115

Schlack, 156

Simonek, Edward, 139

Sun Min Morning Paper, 28 (top)

United Press International, 65, 75, 76, 82, 85, 87, 90, 92, 107, 108, 110, 117, 124, 148, 163, 165, 172

Visiting Nurse Service of New York, 128

Waldorf-Astoria, The, 51

West Point Museum, 78

White House Photo, 32

Illustrated by William Granstaff, Arthur Lutz, Theodore Street, and James Teason